"I worked with Bill for many years and go⸺ sion and expertise for helping churches roll up their sleeves and create community. He has helped people all over the world create greater relational connectedness—and he will help you."

John Ortberg, senior pastor of Menlo Park
Presbyterian Church; author of *Who Is This Man?*

"*The Irresistible Community* describes for us the kind of community we all long to be a part of and how to open it up to the rest of our world. My friend Bill Donahue brilliantly weaves the story of Jesus and his disciples at the Last Supper with important table manners for building genuine community. If you want to lead others beyond believing into true belonging, read *The Irresistible Community.*"

Dave Ferguson, lead pastor of Community Christian Church;
lead visionary for NewThing;
author of *Finding Your Way Back to God*

"We all long for community with others. Sometimes we look for it in the right places. Sometimes we're far off base. But few of us know *why* we so desperately long for connection and belonging. Bill helps us see that those roots start, and find their water, in and through Jesus. As you see Jesus speaking to the disciples in the upper room, you'll hear him speaking to you too. As you hear him speaking to you, you'll hear truth, grace, and love. If you want to pursue a healthy life, pursue it in community. Regardless of where you find yourself in life, Bill's work will shape your thinking."

Steve Gladen, global small group pastor of Saddleback Church;
author of *Small Groups with Purpose*
and *Leading Small Groups with Purpose*

"Once again Bill Donahue brings his vast experience and extensive knowledge of relational dynamics, transformational community, and disciple-making environments to a resource that can change the way we experience church. Anyone who has met Bill knows that his passion for transformational community is irresistible, and this book will make you thirst even more for relationships that matter. Pull up to the table, pass the bread, and dig into the meat of what being the body of Christ is really about. You won't settle for the scraps of mediocre community ever again."

Heather Zempel, discipleship pastor of National
Community Church; author of *Community Is Messy*

"Bill played a big role in helping our church build a thriving group ministry. In one of the training sessions he conducted with our leaders, he walked us through Jesus's vision for community in the upper room discourse. Our leaders caught that vision, and they in turn spread a passion within our church for authentic community comprised of 'table, towel, and truth.' Read this, and you'll find that same passion."

Dr. Tony Evans, senior pastor of Oak Cliff Bible Fellowship;
president of The Urban Alternative

"As much as anyone, Bill Donahue has helped equip the church to make community and small groups values that are able to be replicated anywhere. In *The Irresistible Community: An Invitation to Life Together*, he has served us well again. I read anything and everything I can by Bill Donahue."

Bill Willits, coauthor with Andy Stanley of *Creating Community*

"The term 'community' has become more of a cliché than a way of life. After reading *The Irresistible Community*, I believe deeply that the small group community will recapture what Christian community really is."

Rick Howerton, discipleship and small group
specialist at LifeWay

THE
IRRESISTIBLE
COMMUNITY

THE

IRRESISTIBLE

COMMUNITY

AN INVITATION TO LIFE TOGETHER

BILL DONAHUE

FOREWORD BY DR. HENRY CLOUD

a division of Baker Publishing Group
Grand Rapids, Michigan

Published by Baker Books
a division of Baker Publishing Group
P.O. Box 6287, Grand Rapids, MI 49516-6287
www.bakerbooks.com

Printed in the United States of America

Library of Congress Cataloging-in-Publication Data
Donahue, Bill, 1958–
    The irresistible community : an invitation to life together / Bill Donahue ; foreword by Dr. Henry Cloud.
        pages cm
    Includes bibliographical references.
    ISBN 978-0-8010-1709-4 (pbk.)
    1. Interpersonal relations—Religious aspects—Christianity. 2. Christian life. I. Title.
    BV4597.52.D655 2015
    248.4—dc23   2015007076

Some names and details have been changed to protect the privacy of the individuals involved.

15   16   17   18   19   20   21   7   6   5   4   3   2   1

In keeping with biblical principles of creation stewardship, Baker Publishing Group advocates the responsible use of our natural resources. As a member of the Green Press Initiative, our company uses recycled paper when possible. The text paper of this book is composed in part of post-consumer waste.

To all those who believe
that the life-changing power of a little group,
gathering in the name of Jesus,
can transform the world . . . one life at a time.

Contents

Foreword

Recently I read a review of a book on how people change and overcome longstanding patterns in behavior and life. It caught my attention because it was written by one of the most well-known researchers in the field of change. I tend to gravitate toward books that are empirically based, meaning they have solid research to back them up.

In the synopsis I was captured by one of the arguments of the book, namely, that research has proven there are well-known processes and steps to change, no matter what the change is we are trying to make. I felt a sense of alignment and familiarity with the work the author had assembled. It seemed like a pretty good collection of what the field has learned. Until . . .

As I kept reading, the author's big selling point was finally delivered. It went something like this: "What an exciting time we live in! Science has now shown us that you can change almost anything, if you know how. You don't need treatment, therapy, or other expensive or time-consuming programs. You can change yourself!"

It caught my attention in the same way an oncoming car does. For decades I have seen people change and overcome enormous issues—but virtually never by themselves. It *always* involves others. Yet here was a heralded researcher saying the opposite.

I bought the book.

And—guess what—he was right. The principles he was writing about, and the laws, steps, and stages of the change process were well-documented across many fields of psychology, spirituality and the like. And . . . he was wrong.

Not about the research, steps, and stages of how many problems are changed, but about his central selling point: *you can do it yourself.* In virtually every chapter, every stage, every step of the program, he argued for what he called a "change community." "Put your support and change team together. . . . Tell them what you are struggling with. . . . Get them to hold you accountable, . . . to model for you patterns that you do not know how to do, . . . to teach you what they know, . . . to correct you when you stray." And on and on.

It was a classic "bait and switch."

He told us what we all want to hear: "You can change just by doing these things. Do A, B, and C and your life will be different." But then he slipped in the magic ingredient in each and every A, B, and C: *other people.*

The reality is there is no life change without community.

That is why I am so excited about this book from Bill Donahue. In it he gives us both: the methods and activities of significant life change, *and* the most important tool God uses to help us make life work: relationship.

But he does more. Bill does not just say you have to gather in a church basement, a living room, or a jacuzzi, and "community" will happen and people will be healed. He says there are ways Jesus taught us to be together that produce the change, meaning, and growth we all long for. There are principles that guide the creation, formation, and sustaining of real community, and here he helps us well.

I have had the opportunity to work with Bill on many community-building projects over the last twenty years. I have seen his passion for this work to be real, lived out in his own life, and bear fruit wherever he goes. In this book what you are getting is not just theory, although the principles are sound. It is also field tested and lived out by the author, and those are always the best books.

The message of this book will be helpful both to you and to others you want to help. In Bill's words, "pull up a chair and sit for a while."

Dr. Henry Cloud
Los Angeles, CA
2015

Acknowledgments

For over twenty years I have taught the message of this book around the world, in churches, conference centers, hotel ballrooms, boardrooms, and, perhaps most importantly, in living rooms. All along the way, people shaped my thinking and sharpened my teaching, providing real-life feedback and generously sharing their experiences in community. Together we practiced the Way of Jesus in community, discovering its power, grace, and truth.

Often I found myself to be more of a learner than a teacher, and I wish I could recall all who provided insights, correction, vision, encouragement, and hope along the journey. Indeed, their fingerprints can be found on every page. So, to all who took the risk of leading, building, teaching, and living authentic life in community, patterned after the Master, I say thank you, a thousand times over.

I am forever grateful especially for those who helped me get this message on paper. My amazing wife Gail and my incredible family put up with me when I had to retreat to "the cave" for extended periods of writing, emerging only for food and sleep. They were patient when I was overwhelmed, gracious when I was frustrated, and encouraging when I needed to press on.

Research assistants at TIU made valuable contributions. Alex Gowler provided great insights on Christian community and helped me summarize and articulate the gospel story. Tyler Howell, Derek Caldwell, and Jamie Hudson provided background studies on many of Jesus's followers and the twelve apostles. I am grateful for encouraging feedback on the manuscript from Bill Willits, Rick Howerton, and Steve Gladen, group-life-ministry buddies for life.

I drew much-needed strength from our "familyhood" community, a group of neighbors and friends without whom I would be a bigger mess than I am. And I could never write about community life without gratitude for the Friday morning fellowship of Al, John, Jim, Tom, and Roger.

My agent at WordServe, Greg Johnson, and the staff at Baker Publishing Group collaborated to shape this project when I first shared the idea. My editor, Chad Allen, was patient during the challenging months I suffered with a serious eye condition, and provided essential feedback and counsel regarding the manuscript. Mark Rice, Heather Brewer, and Ruth Anderson brought their marketing savvy to the project and editor James Korsmo, copyeditor Melinda Timmer, and proofreaders Jennifer Jantz Estes and Jess Reimer worked their magic to refine my writing and provide much-needed fluidity and clarity.

For all these, and many unnamed others, I am more than thankful. God has been very good to me.

Introduction

A Personal Invitation

A dozen young men shuffle up the outer stairs to the second-floor doorway. Cautious anticipation and growing uncertainty dominate their emotions. They've been called to attend a very special gathering, an invitation both unexpected and certainly undeserved. They are an unimpressive group, but they arrive eagerly because this is an opportunity they simply cannot refuse.

When you receive an invitation, you size it up, deciding whether to accept or decline. Your response is sometimes determined by the event. If you're invited to the Oscars or the World Series, it would be the eighth deadly sin to refuse such an invitation. In other cases, it's not the event; it's the people. You might get to rub shoulders with a rising pop star, a great actor, an influential business leader, or a political mover and shaker.

Tonight's invitation is one of those "never say no to" offers, especially for this ragtag band of brothers. The main attraction is the host, and every guest considers himself honored to attend. And so they come, a bit disheveled but highly motivated. They long for what you and I long for: a heartfelt connection with genuine friends, a deepening relationship with God, a way to make meaning out of all the confusion and chaos called life.

Crossing the threshold, they pause to stamp the day's dust from their sandaled feet and wipe a day's work from their glistening brows. It is barely dusk as they enter the upper room, but already the walls are awash with shadows, darting and dancing in the flickering candlelight. They are hungry, tired, and eager to get off their aching feet. You know that feeling. Your work is done; your stressful commute is finished; the kids are busy somewhere; and you can barely drag yourself across the room before you plop into a recliner and sigh.

On a nearby table rests a large bowl accompanied by an earthen pitcher filled with warm water. Draped over one corner of the table is a simple, well-worn towel. No one seems concerned that the household servant is absent or that the Master has made special preparations. They rush to their places and recline on several low couches surrounding a modest table, rising barely two feet above the floor. Blankets and pillows cover the couches, creating a comfortable, relaxing environment for a meal. They reach for bread, wine, honey, lentil soup, herbs and spices—a satisfying array of appetizers that quickly brings refreshment and lifts their spirits. In less than an hour the main entrée, a roasted lamb, will be served.

On the surface, everything in the room appears normal, and they are soon caught up in their business-as-usual conversation. But despite the familiarity, they sense something mysterious in the air. No one can put a finger on it. They could see it in the Master's demeanor when he greeted them. They know this feeling. They have experienced it a hundred times over the past three years—the feeling that everything could change in a flash, as it did at the feeding of the five thousand, the healing of the paralyzed boy, and just days ago at the raising of Lazarus.

Anything can happen when Jesus is in the room. You never know what he will say or what he might do. But you can be sure it will be unpredictable, countercultural, and unconventional.

Jesus was an enigma in his time and still is today.

What will Jesus do?

A Night to Remember

On the Jewish calendar, tonight is the fifteenth of Nissan, redemption night, the beginning of Passover. Jews celebrate the night when death and darkness yielded to the unrelenting power of life and light. Over fourteen hundred years ago, the pain, suffering, and oppressive bondage that defined their four-hundred-year existence in Egypt gave way to healing, joy, and freedom. So each year the Hebrews gather to remember.

Tonight—in this upper room—it is a time to remember. Long before the Twelve climbed the stairs, the Master had made the customary preparations for the meal. The day before, paschal lambs were slaughtered at the temple, and families readied themselves for the Passover feast. Jesus made the preparations for their meal, but also for his death. So tonight is not simply the commemoration of an old story; it also marks the beginning of a new one.

At the heart of the celebration is the retelling of the exodus saga, when Jewish families placed lamb's blood on their doorposts so the angel of death would "pass over" their homes. Then the slain lamb was roasted and eaten, along with certain herbs and foods, each symbolic of some aspect of their captivity.

This Thursday evening inaugurates a week-long festival for the Jews, and the meal is the starting point. The instructions given to Moses had been clear: "You shall tell your son on that day, saying, 'It is because of what the LORD did for me when I came out of Egypt'" (Exod. 13:8 NASB).

Only Jesus knows that the new story has already begun, the completion of what the older redemption story only foreshadowed. He "eagerly desired to eat this Passover" (Luke 22:15) with his followers, a clue that something special was in the mix. That he had mentioned leaving (and also his death) just days before this night should have yielded yet another clue. But the disciples were spiritually blind, deaf, and mute. Just like the rest of us.

So in they saunter, unaware that the stage has been set for a drama of another kind. Here they sit, much like we do at an evening meal, with empty bellies and few expectations. On the surface, their mission is as mindless and as narrow as yours and mine can be. Let's eat, retell the Passover story, and hear what the Teacher has to say about our life together.

They hope that future includes the overthrow of Rome, special honors for each of them, and a lifetime membership in this coveted inner circle with Rabbi Jesus. Surely it will be something like that. That much is certain.

Yet nothing is certain. Not when Jesus is around.

Simply Irresistible

The Messiah is on a high-stakes mission, nothing like the one the disciples have envisioned. So he must frame it in simple but compelling terms. In the moments ahead, Jesus will use some very common objects to communicate some very profound mysteries concerning the kingdom of God.

The first is a *table*. So common were tables that people hardly noticed them beyond their basic function as a workbench, a storage facility, or a feeding station. But not after tonight. Tonight the table will become something remarkable. They will never think of a table the same way again. And neither will you.

The second is a *towel*. In a surprising gesture of humility, Jesus will pick up a towel, unmask their self-indulgent thinking, and call them to a radical expression of greatness unlike any the world has seen. From this moment on, whenever they see a common household towel, they will remember. And so will you.

The third, while not an object per se, is the *truth*. In the ancient world, itinerant speakers competed for an audience, passing the hat for a few shekels to feed their families (and avoid an honest day's work). In an era void of television, the internet, coffee shops, and movie theaters, public speakers provided a major form of entertainment and education for a largely illiterate, agrarian culture. Expressions of "truth" were common—but not Jesus's kind of truth. While everyone is yawning at the remarks of yet another soothsayer, Jesus's words awaken the slumbering masses with authority, power, intrigue, mystery, and often bone-crushing reality.

Jesus uses these three common elements—a table, a towel, and the truth—and promises to change the world. He bids his followers to do life together with spiritual depth yet practical wisdom, to become a life-changing community of people who live out his message, encourage his people, and serve his world. This new reality is what we long for. This is what Jesus offers each of us if we are willing to enter the upper room, hear his voice, and respond to his call.

Dietrich Bonhoeffer, in his remarkable book *Life Together*, writes:

> Christian brotherhood is not an ideal which we must realize; it is rather a reality created by God in Christ in which we may participate. The more clearly we learn to recognize that the ground and strength and promise of all our fellowship is in Jesus Christ alone, the more serenely shall we think of our fellowship and pray and hope for it.[1]

You and I are invited by Jesus to enter the upper room to experience fellowship with him, to watch him with the Twelve, and ultimately to experience abundant life together in his name.

His invitation is simply irresistible.

PART 1

Join the Fellowship of the Table

On the first day of the Festival of Unleavened Bread, the disciples came to Jesus and asked, "Where do you want us to make preparations for you to eat the Passover?"

He replied, "Go into the city to a certain man and tell him, 'The Teacher says: My appointed time is near. I am going to celebrate the Passover with my disciples at your house.'" So the disciples did as Jesus had directed them and prepared the Passover.

When evening came, Jesus was reclining at the table with the Twelve.

Matthew 26:17–20

I have eagerly desired to eat this Passover with you before I suffer.

Luke 22:15

We crave connection. We want to be known, cared for, loved, and celebrated. We long to give ourselves to something—to someone—greater than ourselves. We want a little band of brothers and sisters with whom we can do life and mission together. Unfortunately, this sense of connection is elusive for most of us. Either because of choices we've made or circumstances that surround us, we are stuck with ourselves, just ourselves. We stand alone facing the world. And it doesn't feel very good.

We want to be in a place where no one stands alone. We want community. I want community and cannot imagine life without it. I find it in my relationships with my family, in neighborhood gatherings, and in a little band of brothers who huddle together early Friday mornings to share life, talk truth, and encourage one another. These communal relationships call me to a higher place, beyond the world of self and toward God's greater purposes.

Canadian writer Jean Vanier is an expert on the subject of doing life together. As founder of the L'Arche communities for the mentally and developmentally disabled, Vanier has come to understand the absolute necessity of community life for producing durable personal and spiritual growth. Depending on one another for growth and support is essential not only for those with mental challenges or physical disabilities but also for each person who desires to walk in wholeness in the kingdom of God.

Vanier explains why today, more than ever, we long for a rich, deep experience in community:

> When families and tribes were well knit together, people were not lonely. . . . Today the discipline of the family and neighborhood group, with their sense of belonging, have been lost, and personal freedom has increased.
>
> This has led to extreme individualism, but it can also give rise to a deeper search for community and belonging, oriented towards the development of personal consciousness rather than its suppression. . . . "I have come to believe," writes David Clark, "that without a strong sense of community human beings will wilt and begin to die. Community is the foundation of human society, the zenith of interdependence, the epitome of wholeness; in fact, the end of our journeying. As Parker Palmer writes: 'Community means more than the comfort of souls. It means, and has always meant, the survival of the species.' Without a continuing and enriching experience of community, as well as a vision of its glory to keep us moving forward, all of us eventually perish."[1]

The table is perfectly suited to foster authentic Christlike community among people of all ages, backgrounds, creeds, and colors. Jesus was a table builder—literally and spiritually. As the son of Joseph the carpenter, he likely constructed tables of all shapes and sizes, for all purposes and occasions. As the Son of God, a member in the divine community, he invites us to the fellowship of the table. That is what God does for his people, in times of joy, in times of sorrow, and even in our most troubled hours. "You prepare a table before me in the presence of my enemies" (Ps. 23:5). Christ is present at the table. The author of community is both a table maker and a table host.

While an invitation to table fellowship with Jesus sounds wonderful, questions arise:

May anyone sit at the table, or are there some who are excluded?

Are there rules for behavior? How do we treat one another? What kind of environment must be created so that the table experience is meaningful and healthy?

There are different tables for different purposes in the everyday world. Are there different tables for different purposes in the kingdom?

Every table has a story. How do we tell our story in a way that connects with each person's story and, most important, with God's story?

Let's address these questions and grasp the profound transformation that takes place at the table of Jesus and at every table experience we have as we build community together.

Finding Your Place
at the Table

I'm still not sure I fit in, even after three years. The only one who really cares about me—the only one who can forgive my past and the damage I've done—is Jesus. On that day at the tax collector's booth, something about him said "Come" when others clearly bid me "Go," shaking their fists in my face and the dust from their feet.

Tax collectors forage around at the bottom of the religious food chain, but he didn't seem to care. When everyone wanted my head on a platter, he gave me a seat at the table.

I'll never forget it. Jesus sent shock waves through the crowd gathered at the water's edge. I had no business being anywhere near a rabbi, so I kept my distance, hovering nervously at the very back of the large, awestruck crowd whom Jesus was teaching. Though I could barely hear him, I hung on every word. He was stunning.

Later, some young men lowered a paralyzed friend through the roof of the house where Jesus was teaching in a last-ditch attempt to see him healed. And Jesus healed him! That miracle mesmerized the crowd and galvanized Jesus's enemies against him. I would have loved to have seen it up close, but I could never go anywhere near such a house. People despised me. I made my living making other people miserable, taxing many of them beyond what they could bear.

To my shock, Jesus and the crowd headed straight for me after that healing. I can still feel the terror. I could see in their faces they wanted revenge against me, against the authorities, against everything I represented. They had seen a healing; now they wanted a lynching.

He arrived at my booth and paused for what seemed like hours as the crowd fell deadly silent, straining to hear every word. Not one sandal moved. Not one eye blinked.

Then he spoke: "Follow me."

Those two words changed my life, redirected my career, and turned my reputation in the community upside down. They were the two most beautiful words I had ever heard. Somehow I knew he meant something much weightier than two mere words could ever convey. There were no strings attached. No "First beg for mercy, then clean up the moral mess in your life!" None of that.

At first I thought I needed to earn his favor. In my world, everything had to balance. Everything had to net out. If someone gave you something, he wanted something in return. But with Jesus it was all plus and no minus. Just "Follow me! Join my inner circle. Become one of my closest followers and friends." It was not only a shock to me but also a stunning turnaround for onlookers and a slap in the face to self-righteous rule keepers.

If Jesus says I belong, I somehow have to believe it. I'm not sure the others feel the same. Simon the Zealot still scares me.

28

Frankly, I find it hard even to turn my back to him. Yet I also see his heart has been softening. He's not the same as when we first came together. None of us is the same.

The mood tonight is a little more somber than Passover usually is at my home. But for now, I am simply glad to be at the table. It is good to belong.

I am Matthew.

We Long to Belong

Like Matthew, you and I long to belong. We have an innate desire to fit in and feel good about ourselves as we do life in the company of others. The good news is that a virtually unlimited supply of places are at our disposal—from sports clubs to church groups, from neighborhood bars to local business associations. While some expressions of belonging stray far from the norm, they nonetheless function as examples of our craving for community. Examples include the Pork Belly Ventures bicycle club in Iowa, Star Trek conventions, Lord of the Rings fan clubs, and the American Cheese Society. (I wonder if half the members of the cheese society are cardiologists looking for new clients.)

Studies in the social sciences confirm the universality of wanting to belong and the benefits we reap from being part of a meaningful community, especially if faith is a factor. For example, one article notes that people are typically healthier if they are connected to a religious group. "A growing number of studies indicate that people who are religious have better physical and mental health than individuals who are less involved in religion. . . . Although a number of factors are undoubtedly

29

involved, a basic premise . . . is that church-based social support may have something to do with it."[1]

This finding is probably not surprising to Christians. As communal beings made in the image of the Triune God, we long to connect and be known. The more we give ourselves to one another, the more we are fully human, fully alive, and fully expressing who we are as God's unique creation. Said another way, "To be human is to be a participant in a caring community."[2]

But despite our desire to belong and our need for deep relationships, few of us are satisfied with our experience in spiritual community.

So here are a few questions to ponder as we begin our journey:

Do you feel fully alive? Do you find yourself with many acquaintances but very few deep, life-giving relationships?

How would you characterize the quality of your friendships?

Do you have a place to belong?

Has anyone invited you to be part of a community?

Do you believe that you have something to offer a community of people?

If you didn't show up to your regular church service next week, would anyone notice? Would anyone care?

If you are part of a small group that meets regularly, is your motivation to attend tinged with a sense of obligation or guilt or perhaps sheer desperation?

Do you need that group, and does that group need you?

Are you willing to carve out a way of life that involves deep connections with others and greater intimacy with God?

If some of these questions resonate with you, make you uncomfortable, or cause you to reflect deeply about the quality of your life, then keep reading. The level of your spiritual, emotional, and even physical health relates directly to the quality of communal life you experience.

You long for a full and satisfying life. I know I do. And I know that some of life will happen to us and some will happen because of us. We have little or no control over what comes our way—special gifts, joys, people, opportunities, trials, losses, illnesses, accidents, the words and actions of people in our world. But we have been given the responsibility and the opportunity to shape other parts of this life God has given us, including the kind of work we choose, where we live, whom we will marry or whether we will remain single, decisions we make concerning time and money, the people we choose to be part of our lives, and the places where we will belong. It is this last aspect—our communal life—that I want to focus on, because it has so much influence on almost every other area of life.

Let's begin with the primary place where most people find a sense of belonging. It has existed in every culture throughout history and played a significant role in the New Testament church community. Around it people prayed, laughed, cried, learned, played, sang, and—of course—shared daily meals. That place is the table.

Pull Up a Chair

In first-century Jewish culture, people found their place to belong in their family or tribe and as part of the local community. There were really no equivalents to our coffee shops, pubs, community libraries, or local restaurants. People met others in the temple, in a synagogue, or at an outdoor gathering. But most of the time they met in a home, where the table became a symbol of hospitality, acceptance, and friendship. There people found simple food, quality friendship, and occasional fun. Owners of large homes often opened the doors to outsiders after the evening meal so that others could share in the entertainment being provided. They didn't go down to the theater; the theater came to them.

Unfortunately, the table also became a place for separating the powerful, the wealthy, and the beautiful from the weak, the poor, and the undesirable. Seats at the table were assigned by proximity to the host; the more prominent you were, the closer you sat to the host. Many were not invited at all, and some were not even welcome when the doors were opened to the broader community. That list included the usual suspects: lepers, prostitutes, the lame, all kinds of "sinners," and (always near the bottom) tax collectors like Matthew. But Jesus never viewed the table the way others did. Brennan Manning elaborates:

> Through table-fellowship Jesus ritually acted out his insight into the Father's indiscriminate love—a love that causes his sun to rise on bad people as well as good, and his rain to fall on the honest and the dishonest alike (Matt. 5:45). The inclusion of sinners in the community of salvation, achieved in table-fellowship, is the most dramatic expression of the message of the redeeming love of the merciful God. . . .
>
> Jesus' sinner-guests were well aware that table-fellowship entailed more than mere politeness and courtesy; it meant peace, acceptance, reconciliation, fraternity.[3]

Peace, acceptance, reconciliation, brotherhood, and sister-hood are found at the table of Jesus. People desperately want their groups, communities, and churches to feel more like this. The human longing for table fellowship is expressed in every generation. Emerging adults today have a particular desire for smaller expressions of community. In *Finding Faith*, Richard Flory and Donald E. Miller describe this longing:

> The desire for a small community within which they are known, are active, and to which they are responsible is a consistent de-sire for these young people. In some cases this almost becomes a total world, in that they seem to be spending the majority of their time in or at the church. But in general, the desire to be known and to know other parishioners in an intimate way, and to be a part of a spiritual family, is the primary theme expressed.[4]

For Jesus, the great Physician, the table is a healing place—a place for sharing stories, offering hope, extending forgiveness, and pursuing reconciliation. It does not matter who you are or where you're from; all are welcome at Jesus's table. Matthew found a place to belong there, and you will as well. I know some of you cannot believe that. Your experiences at various tables in your life have not always been positive. Sadly, the table has become a place of conflict, isolation, rejection, shame, and even abuse. Whether it's the lunch table at school, the boardroom table at the office, the dinner table at home, or even the fellow-ship table at church, tables can be a pretty scary place to sit. Few tables have anything in common with Jesus's table, and that is heartbreaking.

Today, as he did in the upper room, Jesus comes and changes all of that. He invites us to join him at his table. He extends compassion, provides healing, speaks truth, extends love, creates safety, lends a listening ear, and inspires with challenging ideas.

Will you accept the invitation? For Matthew and the other apostles, it was irresistible.

Dinner for Two . . . and More

My family planned a small surprise for my wife's birthday. We invited her to a local restaurant for dinner. It was not an extravagant or unique dining experience. Actually, it was pretty basic because this was not one of those "significant" birthday years ending in a zero.

We ate a modest, enjoyable meal and arrived home a few minutes before the surprise took place. No exotic jewelry, no cantankerous characters shouting, no fireworks display. The surprise was simply a constant and delightful trickle of close friends arriving for dessert. First one or two entered, then a few more, then another couple, then a handful, and soon about twenty had arrived. Each time someone walked in the door, my wife turned to me, grinned, and gave me that "OK, you little schemer!" sort of look, which I relished throughout the evening. What began as a small gathering became a larger one, much to everyone's delight. It was a joy to honor my amazing wife in this way because relationships are the most profound and beautiful gifts you can give her. (Of course, a little jewelry and a trip to Hawaii would always be welcome!)

Matthew, who felt he belonged nowhere, experienced this same elation when Jesus chose him to join the inner circle, but on a much grander scale. He was so captivated by the invitation to join the new community Jesus was forming that he decided to have a party and invite his friends. While my guest roster for Gail included respectable friends and family, Matthew's list was a who's who of some of the worst characters in the neighborhood. But it did not matter. An invitation to table fellowship with Jesus was simply irresistible. Matthew, who is called Levi in Luke 5:29–32, sent out the invites.

> Then Levi held a great banquet for Jesus at his house, and a large crowd of tax collectors and others were eating with them. But the Pharisees and the teachers of the law who belonged to their sect complained to his disciples, "Why do you eat and drink with tax collectors and sinners?"
>
> Jesus answered them, "It is not the healthy who need a doctor, but the sick. I have not come to call the righteous, but sinners to repentance."

I love that question: "Why do you eat and drink with tax collectors and sinners?" They cowardly asked Jesus's followers because they were unwilling to confront Jesus directly. He provided the answer they probably dreaded: "I have not come to call the righteous, but sinners to repentance."

Imagine Matthew running through the streets inviting his local IRS buddies to dinner (in those days, IRS stood for "Israeli Rip-off Squad"). Each one travels to the dinner party with a mixed sense of wonder, anxiety, excitement, and cautious optimism. Soon these feelings turn from caution to enthusiasm as one by one they discover fellow tax collectors entering the room. There they hang out with Jesus, eating, drinking, and talking with him. Imagine the irony of the moment—the roaring laughter of tax collectors mixing with the rising indignation of the Pharisees. That even tax collectors discovered they had a place at Jesus's side is a beautiful picture of what community life in the kingdom looks like.

There's a seat for everyone at Jesus's table. Everyone is welcome. And Jesus loves every minute of it.

Sorry, but All Our Tables Are Full

Almost any kind of dinner invitation evokes a sense of excitement and joy. That's because it usually means a free meal. But beyond that, it simply feels good to be invited. On the other hand, how painful it is when you're the only one *not* invited; you feel the awkwardness, rejection, shame, and anger welling up inside. Perhaps you lack the proper family pedigree, or come from the wrong ethnic group, or have a poor academic record, or just never got enough votes from "the committee." No one wanted Matthew in the room, let alone at the table—no one except Jesus, who had a particular fondness for sinners in general and wayward tax collectors in particular (the story of Zacchaeus in Luke 19:1–10 comes to mind). Jesus accomplished much of his earthly ministry at tables of every kind, and when he invited Matthew to the table, Matthew was so excited that he just had to throw a dinner party.

Come to the table. Christ has made the preparations. He has given the invitation. And there is a seat waiting for you. Come!

Table Manners

As I look at Jesus, I realize it's been his teaching that has captivated me. When he said "Blessed are the meek," I remember feeling like finally someone understood me and didn't condemn me. Meekness and gentleness (strong traits of mine) are not highly esteemed around this table. The bold bravado of James and John, the sarcasm and cynicism of Thomas and Philip, Peter's clear prominence, and Matthew's steely intelligence seem to take center stage.

Don't get me wrong. People know my personality—it's just that they see it as a weakness. Everywhere I go I am labeled instead of loved. Maybe that's why I have three names: my family name is Jude, and I am the son of James, but most people call me Thaddeus (breast child) or Labbeus (heart child). I've never liked these nicknames; they make me appear weak and childish, not strong and confident. I'm considered the younger one, the little brother who is more pest than partner. Yes, I'm the gentle one, the kind one, the one who tags along with the gang, but I have no real standing. So I've been spending more time with Simon the Zealot to see if that might change my image.

Yet, for some reason it feels different when Jesus looks at me. He sees in my gentleness a great strength. His words on the mountain years ago still ring in my ears: "Blessed are the meek, for they shall inherit the earth." I am hoping this is really true, though right now I don't feel very blessed around this table. And I am not treated like someone who's about to inherit the earth. I want some recognition for my intelligence, inner strength, and spiritual power. But almost no one sees that in me. I want to be someone with impact, someone who is going to make a difference.

But before we take on the whole world, we should probably start here. I think we could all use a little more kindness in our circle. We argue, we debate, and we don't trust one another. Some of these guys hardly say a word, while others can't stop blabbering. Everybody seems to be in it for himself. Amazingly, Jesus treats us like a community, a band of brothers. We surely don't act like one.

I don't know what it's going to take to bring us together, but I sense it's going to be something big, something dramatic, something we'll never forget.

For now, I'll just bide my time. After all, I'm the meek one.

I am Thaddeus.

Table Manners

Many of us grew up with basic rules of etiquette for the dinner table—rules that were usually ratcheted up a notch or two when we were visiting someone else's home or when we dined at a restaurant. Here's a popular list:

"Keep your elbows off the table."

"Don't talk while you're eating."

"Put your napkin in your lap."

"What *goes* in the mouth *stays* in the mouth!"

And the dreaded, "Eat everything on your plate! Remember, there are starving children in Africa."

You remember what it was like. Regardless of what was on the dinner menu, manners mattered. At home or away, you simply did *not* do certain things at the dinner table (like make your sister laugh so hard that milk exploded from her nostrils). And there were other things to which you paid very close attention (like passing everything to the left —or is it to the right? I never remember, so I wait and go with the flow). Eating everything on your plate seemed to trump every other rule, even if brussels sprouts or succotash lay piled in one indigestible heap before your watering eyes. The rule was vigorously enforced, and you broke it at your own risk.

As with a family, all groups and organizations have rules to govern members' behavior. A neighborhood group agrees to certain standards for decorating and landscaping homes in the community. Small groups in churches have covenants that describe the relational climate they want to create. Recovery groups have the twelve steps and the twelve traditions to guide their meetings. Some organizations have a charter. These guidelines are put in place so people know how to treat one another as they form a community. In the process, these "table manners" shape the environment or the culture of the community.

Now that we have a seat at the table and a place to belong, it's important to understand what is expected. Each of us comes to a community with certain assumptions, desires, hopes, and dreams for what it can and should become. But my aspirations and yours may not be the same. Each of us believes we have the best view of what our community should be like; therefore, no one person or subgroup can be allowed to take control, ignoring the contributions and feelings of others. Communities flourish when a spirit of give-and-take characterizes discussions, decision making, and goal setting.[1] While there are dozens of "manners"—values and habits that constitute relational table etiquette—here are five that are indispensible for the enjoyment of fellowship in the name of Jesus.

1. Put Out the Welcome Mat

My family and I spent two weeks traveling in Germany while I was on a speaking tour. From our home base in Heidelberg, we traveled westward to Strasbourg, France, and eastward to Salzburg, Austria. In between, we passed through the stunning landscape of southern Germany, visiting many beautiful towns and villages that dotted the mountainous countryside as well as the world-famous Neuschwanstein Castle in the Bavarian Alps.

My wife observed that one particular family name was very popular in Germany. Like the Joneses or Smiths in the United States or the Anderssons in Sweden, this name appeared often in Germany. "It seems like almost every door in the city has the same family name on it. The Willkomens sure are popular." While my wife is fluent in Spanish, I am the German speaker in our family, so I had to chuckle. "What's so funny?" she asked.

"*Willkomen*," I said, "is German for 'welcome.' They are all saying, 'Welcome to our home.'" We simply had to laugh.

Jean Vanier aptly describes the importance of creating a welcoming environment in a community. We not only welcome one another but also remain open to the possibility that God wants to make room for others at our table. "Welcome is one of the signs that community is alive. To invite others to live with us is a sign that we aren't afraid, that we have a treasure of truth and of peace to share. If a community is closing its doors, that is a sign that hearts are closing as well."[2]

It must grieve the Holy Spirit when a group or a family or a church communicates "not welcome" to those who desperately long for a place at the table. Few things upset Jesus more during his earthly ministry than when self-righteous elites looked down their noses at others. These people were often infuriated when Jesus dined with tax collectors, restored the lame, healed lepers, included women as equals, and reached out to the local riffraff of his day. But welcoming others is the sign that a community is flourishing, growing, and open to strangers. The words of Vanier press the point:

> It is not surprising that Jesus comes under the guise of a stranger: "I was a stranger and you welcomed me." . . . To welcome is to make the stranger feel at home, at ease, and that means not exercising any judgment or any preconceived ideas, but rather giving space *to be.* Once we have made the effort of welcoming and accepting the disturbance, we discover a friend; we live a moment of communion, a new peace; a presence of God is given.[3]

If you attend a recovery group (a group designed primarily to offer support, healing, and growth to people who struggle with addiction or live with those who have addictions), you will likely hear "Keep coming back!" You discover that people sincerely mean it, and you really feel it. I have attended such gatherings and can affirm that I feel welcome no matter what meeting I attend in the area, how regular or erratic my attendance might be, and regardless of whether I contribute much to the conversation. "Great to see you!" say group members with a warm smile. Every time.

At first I doubted their sincerity but later discovered how genuinely glad people were to see me and to see one another. It reminds me of Philip Yancey's column in *Christianity Today* many years ago in which he reflects on what the church can learn from the recovery movement.

> I was struck by one observation from an alcoholic friend of mine. "When I'm late to church, people turn around and stare at me with frowns of disapproval. I get the clear message that I'm not as *responsible* as they are. When I'm late to AA, the meeting comes to a halt and everyone jumps up to hug and welcome me. They realize that my lateness may be a sign that I almost didn't make it. When I show up, it proves that my desperate need for them won out over my desperate need for alcohol."[4]

The table must be a place where grace is abundant. Desperate people need heavy doses of grace, and warmly welcoming them is one of the kindest expressions of grace we can offer. If we are honest, we can acknowledge that we are all desperate people. We may wonder: *What if they really knew me? What if they knew how much I feel like screaming right now—at God, the world, my family? Would they still want me at the table?*

At Jesus's table, the answer is a resounding yes!

2. See the Truth, Be the Truth

In the 1950s and early 1960s, television was filled with feel-good family entertainment, predictable dramas, and lighthearted sitcoms. Programs like *Leave It to Beaver*, *The Ed Sullivan Show*, and the occasional detective drama were safe, uncomplicated, and void of controversy.

This shifted through the late 1960s and 1970s, and by the 1980s and 1990s viewers were exposed to life's harsher realities in programs like the politically incorrect *M*A*S*H* and the trauma-filled *ER*, where scenes were bloody and characters were complicated. Episodes rarely ended with happy people living problem-free lives. This set the stage for an onslaught of "reality" shows in the past fifteen to twenty years, most finding their roots in MTV's *Real World* and the iconic *Survivor*.

While some viewers are becoming weary of the plethora of such shows, it is clear that the Ozzie-and-Harriet genre of the 1950s left much to be desired and was even misleading about the complexities of life. Our hunger for authenticity likely stems from our conscience and sense of what's right and fair. As a result, we cry out, "There's something wrong here, and I don't like it!"

Authenticity—being true to self and others—matters when Jesus is at the table. He never shies away from declaring truth about himself, his Father, or life in the world. "In this world you will have trouble," he declares. "But take heart! I have overcome the world" (John 16:33). Jesus was clearly not a typical motivational speaker. "In this world you will have trouble" is not the best way to launch a pep rally—unless you quickly add, "But don't worry! I will remove from your life all the trouble in this world!" Now we're getting somewhere. That'll get the crowd pumped! The all-powerful Jesus has spoken, and he will take all the evil away.

Not exactly.

After the reminder "You will have trouble," we hear instead, "I have overcome the world." I am not sure the disciples were thrilled to hear that. Perhaps they were thinking: *OK, that's great for you, Jesus. But when do we overcome the world? Please get us out of this crazy place! Or at least overrun the Romans and spare us from the Pharisees. We need more than 'Take heart!' in order to win this battle. Frankly, most of us just lost heart.*

You and I have been there. We do not often like the reality we face. Our lives "woulda coulda shoulda" been better than this. If God had simply done what we asked and expected, everything would be different. Why can't he meet our expectations? When is he going to show up? That voice from within sounds so familiar, maybe a lot like the beginning of Psalm 13. Like the psalmist, we hear it ringing louder and louder in our ears as our frustration mounts:

> How long, LORD? Will you forget me forever?
>   How long will you hide your face from me?
> How long must I wrestle with my thoughts
>   and day after day have sorrow in my heart?
> How long will my enemy triumph over me?

Look on me and answer, LORD my God.

Give light to my eyes, or I will sleep in death,

and my enemy will say, "I have overcome him,"

and my foes will rejoice when I fall. (Ps. 13:1–4)

When I cry out, "How long, Lord? Will you forget me forever?" it means that I live among the broken, needy, wounded, and scared, just like David did. My emotions are raw, my fears debilitating, my questions unanswerable. In these moments when I name reality, I feel so alone. So I turn toward others, especially when I feel as if God has turned away.

Relationships at the table come alive when spiritual realities in our lives are identified and embraced. Soon we observe that God is at work behind the scenes doing more than we could ever ask or think to ask for. His gifts may be hidden (at least from our earthly vision), but despite our blindness, Jesus generously gives us more than we can imagine. Spiritual realities are present, and we must train ourselves to see them. Here are a few to lay hold of:

Jesus declared victory over the evil forces of the world, even before going to the cross. The victory is won (John 16:33).

Through Christ, God has given us everything we need for life in the world. Not partial help. Everything (2 Pet. 1:3–4).

He promises to be with us as we join his redemptive mission of sharing the good news with the world. We are not alone (Matt. 28:18–20).

We have his Holy Spirit to give us real power, strength, courage, passion, and truth as we carry out our life and work (John 16:5–11).

Our challenges are light compared to eternity and the glory we experience with God working in us. Soon it will be over (2 Cor. 4:17).

The list could go on and on. Kingdom realities abound, declaring who we are and what the world is really like. Our ability to be authentic at the table is a direct result of how we see the world. The truths above provide a small sample of what God is doing and has done for his people. They give us perspective so we do not have to fear the world or ignore the realities of it. M. Scott Peck affirms this:

> The more clearly we see the reality of the world, the better equipped we are to deal with the world. The less clearly we see the reality of the world—the more our minds are befuddled by falsehood, misperceptions and illusions—the less able we will be to determine correct courses of action and make wise decisions.[5]

We boldly face reality when we are clear about who we are in Christ—loved, chosen, redeemed, blessed, empowered, gifted, free, and fully alive. At the same time, we must acknowledge that we are also needy, broken, scarred, vulnerable, and weak. So we bring our true selves to the table, understanding the real world in which we live. We do not have to deny what is happening around us. We come with confidence and without fear because Jesus has overcome the world.

Once we acknowledge our desperation, pain, and brokenness, we can join with poet-King David and complete Psalm 13. "How long, LORD?" (v. 1) still remains true, but now we have a new perspective. Our confusion and fear persist but are covered, enveloped in a greater reality. We are able to declare our confidence in the God who is love and who has done great things in and for us. As David proclaims (and we echo today), we trust in God despite the pain of our present reality.

> But [even though my enemy seeks to swallow up my
> life] I trust in your unfailing love,
> my heart rejoices in your salvation.
> I will sing the LORD's praise,
> for he has been good to me. (Ps. 13:5–6)

We can *see* the truth, and we can *be* the truth.

3. Be Someone Others Can Trust

When a table is characterized by mutual trust among its members, we can reveal the most tender and vulnerable parts of ourselves without fear or worry. When I share feelings, fears, disappointments, and desires with others, I am offering a gift, and that gift is my life story. In effect, I am asking others to steward that story with love, care, and respect. I am placing the most fragile yet valuable parts of myself in their hands. I am hoping that trust will not be broken. In chapter 4, I will talk in depth about how our stories shape our table, but first trust (an essential table manner) must be cultivated.

Proverbs 11:13 declares, "A gossip betrays a confidence, but a trustworthy person keeps a secret." How many of you have shared a private prayer request with a friend only to have your request go public without your permission? This is a real trust buster in community. Whether shared out of voyeuristic passions, malicious intent, or sheer ignorance, gossip produces shame in the victim, arrogance in the tattletale, and division in the group.

Trust comes as a result of "welcome" and "truth" working together. Welcome (grace in action) and truth (reality revealed) form the backbone of trust. We welcome one another in grace, offering forgiveness, hope, acceptance, and belief. We see and embody the truth about God, self, and the world. When these two join forces, trust thrives.

When trust is shared and growing at the table, the result is powerful.

A young woman confides in others about her eating disorder, finding gracious responses, comfort, and offers of help.

A couple shares their fears about their pregnancy, admitting that the miscarriage two years ago still plagues their thoughts. Others rally with prayer, hugs, empathy, hope, and promises to be present every step of the way.

A middle-aged man tells friends he is starting a new business after being downsized out of a job but admits this is a big leap and he is insecure. At the table, he sees smiles and hears offers of help with his business plan and office space, wise counsel, wisdom from experienced marketplace people, and real truth about the challenges he is likely to face.

At a trust-filled table, no one worries about inappropriate responses, broken confidences, or jealousies. Trust built on welcome and truth creates a safe environment where words flow smoothly from each person and listening is deep, caring, and fully engaged. Members find fear and worry replaced by mutual encouragement, freedom, and serenity.

When we trust, we reflect the character of God. His faithfulness—his trustworthiness—is the bedrock of our faith. If he cannot be trusted, we are doomed. Listen to the Bible speak of this trust (there are sixty references in the psalms alone).

> Some trust in chariots and some trust in horses,
>> but we trust in the name of the LORD our God.
>> (Ps. 20:7)

> In God, whose word I praise—
> in God I trust and am not afraid.
>> What can mere mortals do to me? (Ps. 56:4)

> Let the morning bring me word of your unfailing love,
>> for I have put my trust in you.
> Show me the way I should go,
>> for to you I entrust my life. (Ps. 143:8)

> Trust in the LORD with all your heart
>> and lean not on your own understanding;
> in all your ways submit to him,
>> and he will make your paths straight. (Prov. 3:5–6)

Our God is trustworthy. But the more astounding truth is that he has placed great trust in us. He has entrusted us with the good news of the gospel (1 Thess. 2:2), has trusted us as partners in the ministry of reconciliation (2 Cor. 5:18–20), and has given us the privilege of caring for his most precious possession—people! There are over twenty-five "one another" statements in the Bible such as "love one another," "pray for one another," "serve one another," and "carry one another's burdens."⁶ Trust is at the heart of God's character and mission, and we are his fellow workers in making mutual trust a reality.

We cultivate trust at the table when we give people the benefit of the doubt, follow through with our promises, share the responsibilities of community life, own our mistakes, and relinquish our desire to control others. If I share something about myself—trusting others with a part of me—trust grows. Because they sense that I trust them with my feelings and thoughts, they in turn can trust me with theirs. In so doing, our overall trust of one another deepens. Hence, we build trust by trusting.

Put your trust in one another and strengthen your table.

4. Let Go, and Let Go Again

Jean Vanier is again instructive:

> When we accept that we have weaknesses and flaws, that we have sinned against God and against our brothers and sisters, but that we are forgiven and can grow towards inner freedom and truer love, then we can accept the weaknesses and flaws of others. They too are forgiven by God and are growing towards the freedom of love. We can look at all men and women with realism and love. We can begin to see in them the wound of pain that brings up fear, but also their gift which we can love and admire. We are all mortal and fragile, but we are all unique and precious. There is hope; we can all grow towards greater freedom. We are learning to forgive.⁷

Few experiences restore joy, hope, and freedom at the table more than giving and receiving forgiveness. How many times do we hear phrases like "I'll never forgive him," or "I just can't let that go," or "She's going to regret she did that to me for the rest of her life." It's hard to let go when someone or something has hurt us. The physical, emotional, and psychological damage may be severe. We cannot imagine just simply forgiving the perpetrator of our pain. And so our pain becomes our prison. Our unforgiving spirit becomes our undoing. No one knows this truth better than Anthony Colón.

Twenty-one years ago Michael Rowe killed Wilfredo Colón. Today, Wilfredo's younger brother, Anthony, who was 15 at the time of the murder, is friends with Wilfredo's killer after forgiving him for the murder.

In 2006, Anthony Colón was visiting a friend who was serving time at the Eastern Correctional Facility in Ulster County, New York, when he recognized Rowe across the room. Colón got up, walked towards Rowe with an outstretched hand and a smile on his face, and said, "Brother, I've been praying for you. I forgave you. I've been praying I would see you."

On June 13, 1992, 17-year-old Wilfredo Colón was shot thirteen times by three young men who were fighting over drug dealing turf. The corner on which he was shot was outside his family's apartment located at the East River Projects in Manhattan. Michael Rowe was one of those three men. . . .

Rowe was arrested eight months after the shooting. . . . He served 20 years in prison and was released the first week of April 2013.

While in prison, Rowe earned a masters degree, married his long-time girlfriend, and had three children.

Anthony Colón also married and had two children. The most significant change in his life came two years after his brother

Wilfredo's death—he became a Christian. . . . All of his rage was consumed by the healing of the Bible. He prayed and ultimately forgave the men who killed his brother.[8]

It may be hard to believe, but Rowe and Colón are friends today. They are living proof that it is possible to reach the point of letting go. The popular phrase "Let go and let God" is the life mantra of many who declare this reality for themselves each day. Behind this slogan is the idea of trusting God with the affairs of our lives and relinquishing our desire to manipulate, control, and orchestrate the future. It applies to forgiveness too.

I find it takes a double effort to fully let go of the things I want to hold on to. I must let go, and let go again (and again). It's easy for me to say, "I forgive you," but it's difficult for me to practice forgiveness. I hold on to things I want to hold against others. Truth be told, I keep a list. I'm tempted to ignore or dishonor the pure intent of true, lasting, Christlike love—a love that "keeps no record of wrongs" (1 Cor. 13:5). And so I must let go, and let go again.

Vanier notes:

In spite of all the trust we may have in each other, there are always words that wound, self-promoting attitudes, situations where susceptibilities clash. That is why living together implies a cross, a constant effort, an acceptance which is daily, and mutual forgiveness. . . . To forgive is also to understand the cry behind the behavior. . . . Perhaps they feel rejected. Perhaps they feel that no one is listening to what they have to say or maybe they feel incapable of expressing what is inside them. . . . To forgive is also to look into oneself and to see where one should change, where one should also ask for forgiveness and make amends.[9]

A culture of forgiveness makes any community irresistible. I desperately long to be part of a group, team, church, business, or board where people genuinely let go and let God do his transforming work at the soul level. We let go of the need to win, the temptation to shame others, and the constant drive of self-promotion. By grace, we exchange these destructive tendencies for other-mindedness and thus free one another—and ourselves—from the deadly plague of unforgiveness.

When we extend forgiveness we are giving an unexpected (and, some might argue, undeserved) gift to others. But we are doing something else as well. In some profound and mysterious way, this gift we give also becomes a gift to us, because the cost of not forgiving is simply too high. Shame never leads to freedom, and self-righteousness softens no hearts. When we forgive, we make a decision to free ourselves from harboring resentments and passing judgments. Forgiveness never means we ignore destructive patterns in others that must be confronted or pretend we have not been hurt by the actions of others. It simply means we submit again to God, who is in control. When I refuse to forgive, I am allowing my hatred of others to control my thoughts and attitudes. To forgive means to take back that control and find freedom.

Therefore, as God's chosen people, holy and dearly loved, clothe yourselves with compassion, kindness, humility, gentleness and patience. Bear with each other and forgive one another if any of you has a grievance against someone. Forgive as the Lord forgave you. And over all these virtues put on love, which binds them all together in perfect unity. (Col. 3:12–14)

Forgiveness, rooted in our own need to be forgiven and made possible by the love of Christ in us, brings unity to the table.

5. Strive for Progress Not Perfection

This is another one of my favorite slogans.[10] Catchy and deceptively simple, the phrase "progress not perfection" reveals a deep and profound theology of spiritual growth. I find the phrase a refreshing alternative to the "work until everything is perfect and then you'll earn my approval" thinking that we encounter far too often each day.

This table manner is usually not among the top five on most people's lists. Grace, forgiveness, love, laughter, listening, kindness, and similar virtues are often at the forefront. In my opinion, however, we neglect this table manner at our own peril. While the others rightly focus on our *demeanor* at the table, "progress not perfection" focuses on our *direction*. A community that makes no progress has no purpose, no goal, and the spiritual life clearly has goals, both individual and communal. Some believe progress is too difficult to measure and thus avoid discussing or pursuing it, lest they careen down the slippery slope toward legalism and self-righteousness. I believe this fear is unfounded.

Groups of all kinds need to focus their efforts toward some goal. It might be growth in relational skills, the study of a topic, service to the broader community, or provision of a place for personal reflection and connection with God. In order for progress to be seen and growth to be celebrated, there must be a reason to gather.

The Bible prods us toward progress, so any community worth its salt should do the same and should (like Jesus) make it a priority. A number of verses speak to spiritual progress in the faith.

There are blessings for obedience as we grow in our faith and pass it along to our children. Moses says, "These are the commands, decrees and laws the LORD your God directed me to teach you to observe in the land that you are crossing the Jordan to possess, so that you, your children and their children after them may fear the LORD your God as long as you live by keeping all his decrees and commands that I give you, and so that you may enjoy long life" (Deut. 6:1–2).

Psalm 1 teaches that our relationships and practices matter: "Blessed is the one who does not walk in step with the wicked . . . but whose delight is in the law of the LORD." Then we will grow and produce fruit like a tree planted by streams of water (Ps. 1:1–3).

God gives us specific roles to play in the church, equipping us for works of service so that "we will grow to become in every respect the mature body of him who is the head" (Eph. 4:13–15).

Paul says his goal is to "present everyone fully mature in Christ," adding that "to this end I strenuously contend with all the energy Christ so powerfully works in me" (Col. 1:28–29). This is a beautiful picture of how Jesus gives us the energy we need to perform our disciple-making labor in his kingdom.

Paul tells young co-worker Timothy to "pursue righteousness, godliness, faith, love, endurance, and gentleness" (1 Tim. 6:11). Progress takes effort.

"Train yourself to be godly" (1 Tim. 4:7). Spiritual training is required for spiritual progress to result.

The writer of Hebrews exhorts his audience to move beyond drinking infant's milk (basic teachings for new believers) and to begin eating solid food (deeper truths and righteous living) so that they will become mature in the faith (Heb. 5:12–14).

"And let us consider how we may spur one another on toward love and good deeds" (Heb. 10:24). We encourage one another to make progress as we serve and love others.

The table is a healing place. There we express needs and extend hope, share struggles and pray prayers, listen deeply and laugh loudly. But we do these things (and much more) to make spiritual and relational progress. Faith is a journey, to be sure; it is not a straight and easy path. While there are rest stops along the way for refreshment and renewal, we nonetheless are called by Christ to make headway.

Our progress requires effort. Some balk at the mention of this word, eager to remind us that it is God who does the work. True, nothing can be done without God's power and the Spirit's guidance. Jesus clarifies that he can do nothing without his Father's strength and wisdom (John 5:19, 30). Likewise, we can do nothing apart from Christ's help (John 15:5), but that does not mean we do nothing. We definitely do something. We were created to work in the world in the name and power of Christ

(Eph. 2:10). God calls us to be partners, not puppets. We work because God is at work in us. His work makes our work possible. He does not do the work for us but rather in us, which requires effort on our part.

Listen to Paul: "Therefore, my dear friends, as you have always obeyed—not only in my presence, but now much more in my absence—continue to *work out your salvation* with fear and trembling, for it is God who works in you to will and to act in order to fulfill his good purpose" (Phil. 2:12–13, italics mine).

I was with Dallas Willard in Southern California in January 2013, just months before he passed away, when he taught, "God is not opposed to effort, but he is opposed to earning." Jesus, Paul, and Peter would agree. Effort is not evil. Listen to their exhortation (italics mine):

Jesus: "*Make every effort* to enter through the narrow door, because many, I tell you, will try to enter and will not be able to" (Luke 13:24).

Paul: "Let us therefore *make every effort* to do what leads to peace and to mutual edification" (Rom. 14:19); "*Make every effort* to keep the unity of the Spirit through the bond of peace" (Eph. 4:3).

The writer of Hebrews: "Let us, therefore, *make every effort* to enter that rest, so that no one will perish by following their example of disobedience" (4:11); "*Make every effort* to live in peace with everyone and to be holy; without holiness no one will see the Lord" (12:14).

Peter: "For this very reason, *make every effort* to add to your faith goodness; and to goodness knowledge" (2 Pet. 1:5);

"Therefore, my brothers and sisters, *make every effort* to confirm your calling and election. For if you do these things, you will never stumble" (2 Pet. 1:10); "So then, dear friends, since you are looking forward to this, *make every effort* to be found spotless, blameless and at peace with him" (2 Pet. 3:14).

Progress requires effort but not our effort alone. God is at work in us, and we have the mutual support and encouragement of others at the table. We do this together, in community. That's the beauty of table fellowship. We persevere in prayer, labor in service, struggle in pain, work out our salvation, and strive for unity.

Manners Matter

These five table manners will help to create an environment in which the Holy Spirit does his transforming work. Manners at the table determine our experience at the table. When they are followed with joy and freedom, a culture for authentic relationships is created. We find a new way of being together in our community of friends and a more confident way to be in the world. What we practice at the table we carry into the world. What we learn about God, ourselves, and others at the table prepares us for reentry into the challenges and complexities of life.

Our place at the table is safe and secure, and table manners are in place so we can function with health and strength. As we do, we discover that our community does not look and act the same during every season, and we discover the value each member brings to the community, regardless of their weaknesses and imperfections.

Our church has a ministry among the physically, mentally, and emotionally challenged called Special Friends. Recently, we partnered with the Penguin Project, an organization that gives young people with special needs an opportunity to participate in the performing arts.[11] I cannot begin to tell you what it was like to see thirty young people with an array of challenges bring their unique gifts to the stage. Despite their afflictions with cerebral palsy, Down syndrome, autism, and hearing impairments, they burst forth with disarming humor, joyous singing, unbridled dancing, and extremely good acting. It was one of the most edifying experiences I have ever had.

We all come to the table as our unique selves with unique goals and desires. The table may take on new meaning and purpose during each phase of life or even from week to week. Depending on what we need to accomplish and what is required for our lives, the table may function differently each time we meet. But with our table manners firmly in place, we can provide the kind of table each of us needs.

What kind of table do you need?

Choose a Table,
Any Table

I like information, details, clarity. I tend to think more with my head than with my heart. As I sit here looking around the table, I wonder what's going on. I wish Jesus would just get to the point. Sometimes it all seems so mystical and spiritual and ethereal to me, especially when John is talking. It's hard for me to accept the spiritual realities of what Jesus is doing. It's so much clearer to me when there is something I can see and feel and touch.

I've been this way since my childhood in Bethesda, growing up not far from Andrew and Peter. I identify more with them than anyone else here. I like things straight, focused on the facts. It was a no-brainer for me to follow Jesus when he first called. I'd studied the Torah enough to know right away that he was the one Moses was talking about. Can't the others see that? Even the prophets are clear. This one from Nazareth, the son of Joseph, is surely the conquering Messiah and Jewish liberator.

But as I listen to Jesus, I wonder if this is the same person I met almost three years ago. Now he's saying things like, "My children, I will be with you only a little longer. You will look for me, and just as I told the Jews, so I tell you now: Where I am going, you cannot come." Why all the mystery? I'm sure John loves this spiritual guessing game, but it's not for me. Judas is also getting irritated. Frankly, he can be a shifty character at times. Let's face it. We're a mixed-up bunch.

I really need Jesus to guide me. But I don't understand what he's saying, and I don't know where we're going. If he would just show us the Father, that would be great. That's all I need: simple, straight, down-to-earth. Thomas would understand my reasoning. He shares my concerns. He knows it doesn't all add up either.

It's not as though I don't believe in spiritual realities or miracles. After all, I was there when Jesus fed the five thousand. But I tend to be direct. When Jesus asked, "Where shall we buy bread for all these people to eat?" I assumed a direct question deserved a direct answer. I said, "Eight months' wages would not buy enough bread for each one to have a bite!" Sure, I was being sarcastic, but it seemed so obvious that we were underresourced and overwhelmed. How was I to know he was testing me? I suppose after he healed the paralytic at the Sheep Pool I should have had more confidence. But everything seems to be unraveling, and half the people in the room cannot see it.

This group began with great potential, exciting teaching, fun road trips, and plenty of time with Jesus. Now everywhere we go people loathe him, despise us, and hate living under this oppressive Roman regime. Something has to change. We just need to get our hands on the right information.

I am Philip.

The Organic Nature of the Table

When we find our place at the table and practice the habits that make a gathering thrive, our community may take on many forms and expressions. This is because a community is organic and adaptive, changing shape and form as needed, responding to the changing needs and personalities of its members. Newcomers arrive while others depart. Every change in membership brings a new dynamic to navigate.

We may all be created equal, but all tables are not. Each has a different purpose, culture, and operating guidelines. I have come to accept that I need a variety of table-fellowship experiences in my life. You likely do as well.

Philip is a case in point. He desires a different kind of fellowship, a nostalgic return to the early days when being with Jesus was dynamic and carefree. We each have a bit of Philip in us. Once we belong to a group or a community that we enjoy, we never want to leave it and pray it never changes.

As we mature, however, we realize that in order to embrace everyone at the table, we must be willing to release the grip on our personal agenda and see what is best for the community. When we enter into significant relationships with others, we find that a number of factors influence how we grow as individuals and as a community. Our needs, the changing seasons of life, the spiritual maturity of others, our goals, the flow of people in and out of our lives, the crises and problems that arise unexpectedly, and dozens of other factors come into play. Life at the table can be complex and challenging to navigate.

Let's consider some of the tables we encounter almost every day, reflecting on how they represent ways we experience community and how they catalyze our growth in Christ, help to ground us in the gospel, and facilitate our communal life with others.

The Kitchen Table: When You Need to Feel at Home

How many times have you been in someone's home or apartment and suddenly found yourself (and everyone else!) assembled in the kitchen, regardless of its size. Soon people are gathering at the kitchen table, long before the meal is served. Unlike the formality we might experience at the dining room table (think special occasions like Christmas dinner or a business meeting at a restaurant), the kitchen table begs people to pull up a chair and start talking.

There's just something about the kind of fellowship we enjoy around a kitchen table—a certain charm we perceive that makes us feel comfortable and at home. Here we experience unbridled laughter, shed a few tears, share stories, reflect on the day's drama, and are keenly aware that we are accepted.

Even when we are not sitting at the table, a kind of kitchen table fellowship takes place just by being in the room. At our home, we have the hardest time getting people out of our kitchen. It is not very large or fancy, and it's certainly not designed for twenty loud, boisterous people talking and shouting like they're on the dance floor at an Italian wedding! Despite encouraging folks to move to other rooms filled with comfortable chairs and cozy couches, they'd rather plop their derrieres on the countertop, crowd themselves into a corner, or squeeze in that cramped three-foot space directly between the center island and our refrigerator. Why?

Food.

Food is the great equalizer and potent peacemaker. When there's food in the room, rich and poor, black and white, young and aged, avant-garde and old guard have something in common. Food is the metaphor Jesus uses when he wants to describe deep oneness and relationship. He implores, "Listen! I am standing and knocking at your door. If you hear my voice and open the door, I will come in and *we will eat together*" (Rev. 3:20 CEV, italics mine). Jesus doesn't simply invite you to *his* table. He's willing to come to *your* table and build a relationship with you.

In the kitchen table atmosphere of the upper room, the disciples greet one another, grab some appetizers, and talk about the day's work and latest news. They feel welcome and grateful. Despite the occasional friction among them, here they feel at home and share much in common. A sense of belonging emerges.

Jesus asks little from this group as they gather, allowing them time to simply be present and enjoy fellowship with one another. It is a gift they do not fully grasp. Perhaps we do not either. Have you ever been in a kitchen-table gathering but someone wants to turn it into a political debate, a sales meeting, or—worse yet—a theological argument? Simply connecting around food feels too unstructured and unproductive for some people. Some of us are impatient and, like Philip, begin wondering, *When does the program get started? Let's get to the point and get this over with.*

Think of the places where you gather and the people with whom you gather. Is there room for some table fellowship around the kitchen table? Or has the fast-food pace of life robbed you of some much-needed unstructured time?

I meet with a neighborhood men's group on Friday mornings to process life together in a spirit of grace and truth. We have our share of debates and disagreements and often wrestle with some of life's biggest questions. Along the way we've tackled some tough topics: religious pluralism, divorce, human sexuality, legalism, partisan politics, leadership failures, poverty, injustice, human rights, fiscal policy, global economics, racism, abortion, greed, alcoholism, abuse, church scandals, and school restructuring, to name a few. But one thing we can count on each week is feeling at home. It grieves me to miss a Friday morning with these guys. We've locked arms for many years now, walking with one another through life's most difficult storms and celebrating some incredible highs. Here we find accountability, friendship, hope, sacrificial service, challenge, laughter, tears, grace, truth, and love. We'd give our lives for one another and for one another's families.

But it all starts the same each week: at the kitchen table (quite literally), where we grab some coffee and a pastry or fruit and jump right into the conversation. We've become a band of brothers meeting in the name of Jesus, lifetime members in the fellowship of the kitchen table.

The Conference Table: When There's a Decision to Be Made

There is a time for everything—a time to hang out in the kitchen with family and friends and a time to gather information and make decisions. When a community has a problem to work through or a decision to make, the mood shifts, the focus changes, and we sit down at the conference table. The decisions we make will make us bitter or better. We can deal with our problems or deny them.

Making decisions without engaging our community is like buying our first used car without a grown-up around. Experience matters. Wisdom is essential. Insight and discernment are indispensible.

Some label this kind of table a "personal board of directors," while others may refer to it as a "life process group." The Quakers, a prominent religious community in the sixteenth through eighteenth centuries that is still active today, use something they call a "clearness committee" whenever someone needs to confer with others about a potentially life-altering decision. The decision maker sits facing her close friends and wise elders as they pepper her with thoughtful questions. No advice giving allowed. No judgmental comments or shame-filled accusations. Just a couple of hours filled with good, honest, thoughtful, provocative questions—the kind that cause you to weigh the impact of the choice at hand, with all of the possible options and potential consequences. Without a clearness committee or something similar, we glibly ignore wise counsel at our own peril. I know. Once I almost did.

In the midst of building my coaching and consulting practice, I was invited to join a larger consulting organization—at a substantial salary. Despite being a young, emerging business, it had experienced rapid growth and boasted a list of satisfied clients. I knew some of the principals involved and had heard good things about their work. But it had been a couple years since I had interacted closely with them, and the decision to join would mean closing my fledgling start-up to jump in with them. As I shared the opportunity with close friends in my little community, I expected to hear, "That sounds great!" Instead, they expressed modest concerns and began to wave some yellow warning flags.

How could they? Here was a strong opportunity, a ground-floor chance to help build a new clientele, leverage my areas of expertise, and receive a steady salary instead of riding the income roller coaster typical of the early years of a start-up. I knew the people; I understood the market; and it was the kind of entrepreneurial work I enjoyed. I would have the freedom to build the company plus the resources of an established organization. Only one thing stood in the way: my conference table community was pushing back at every turn.

Though we did not meet formally as a group, these men and women (including my discerning wife) asked many hard questions:

Will this allow you to use your teaching gifts?

Will you be part owner or be treated more like a contract worker? Is there a stock option?

How much travel will it entail? Does the amount of travel allow you to keep the priorities you've set for your wife, kids, community service, and personal growth?

How stable is the organization? How about revenues and expenses? How do the balance sheet and cash flow statement look? Will you have a budget to manage?

Is there administrative help for you—you've said that's a real weakness for you. Can you hire someone?

How are decisions made, and will you have strategic input when they are made? Will you be able to use your strategic-thinking ability?

What do people say who have worked with them?

This represents just the initial salvo in a barrage of questions they fired at me. Frankly, I was tempted to ignore most of them. After all, everything seemed so right: the timing was perfect, the location convenient (just up the street from my current office), and the opportunity ripe. Sure, I could see some yellow caution flags, but nothing that I couldn't overcome or fix. For months we discussed the prospect of a working relationship, but the more we talked, the more it just didn't feel right. Input from friends and family concurred. I could never put my finger on exactly what made me feel so uncomfortable and uncertain, but things just fizzled out.

Sadly, the organization was forced to shut down eighteen months later. The employees either were dismissed or struggled through the tough months of transition. The owner had to start over. I shudder as I reflect on how close I came to working there. To gather at the conference table, both formally and informally, made all the difference in the world, and I thank God today for the wisdom and input of my community.

When it's time to confer and decide, we need a trusted community who will sit around the conference table with us. Yogi Berra famously quipped, "When there's a fork in the road, take it!" That's always good for a laugh, but it's bad advice. Discerning and listening together is the best way to go when a decision needs to be made and one of the most treasured gifts you can offer one another.

Is it time to gather at the conference table? I wouldn't miss it if I were you.

The Negotiation Table: When You're in a Battle

Here's a riddle: enduring marriages require it; successful businesses demand it; politicians thrive on it; but few people are prepared for it. What is it?

Conflict.

Unfortunately, there are too many empty seats at the negotiation table. Many people avoid the invitation to pull up a chair because the idea of negotiation conjures up images of arguing, name-calling, backbiting, power-brokering, and give-and-take battles that are all "take" and no "give." Most of us would rather wait until the war is over or let others do the dirty work.

How boring. You're missing all the action and all the potential for character growth. You can read every textbook on group communication and discover that they all say the same two things. First, conflict in groups is inevitable. Second, conflict can lead to growth (both for the community as a whole and for the individuals in the community) *if handled correctly*.[1]

A good friend of mine provides legal services to groups who cannot get along. Believe it or not, most of his work is with churches—not because they are filled with mean-spirited people trying to destroy one another (though there are a few) but because the issues are so complex. Church battles can leave behind a destructive wake of relational fallout, and some churches never heal. The Bible urges us not to take one another to court but

70

rather to work things out; some call it "biblical conciliation," and it is a difficult path to navigate.

Once my friend described a particular conflict he was mediating between two churches in a denomination. A heated theological disagreement, relational infighting, financial misunderstanding, and organizational chaos all came to a boil, with the lid tightly fastened! I said, "Wow! Looks like this thing could blow up at any moment!," to which he replied, "I know. And I love it!" *Really? Is he kidding? Tolerate it, maybe. But love it?*

I've learned that he "loves it" not simply because he's gifted at working in these volatile situations. He loves it because he loves people and he loves peacemaking. For him, negotiation is more than the art of securing a win-win outcome. Negotiation makes reconciliation possible, resulting in restored relationships, renewed commitment to grace and truth, and repentant hearts.

At the negotiation table participants say, "Let's talk this through and set things right again. Our relationships matter, these friendships matter, and this community matters." When conflict starts boiling, we don't put a lid on it. Instead, we turn down the heat and turn up the dialogue so that cooler minds can prevail.

Negotiating is not the hard part. The difficult part is being willing to honestly work through a process with integrity to the very end. But it's worth it, and our commitment to authentic community demands it. Larry Crabb puts it this way:

> Conflict is a problem only spiritual community can handle. . . . The difference between spiritual and unspiritual community is not whether conflict exists, but is rather in our attitude toward it and our approach to handling it. When conflict is seen as an

opportunity to draw more fully on spiritual resources, we have the makings of a spiritual community.[2]

Sitting at the negotiation table may feel uncomfortable. Emotions around the circle may be intense, simmering just beneath the surface and easily brought to a full boil. Don't let that happen. Be courageous enough to pull up a seat at the negotiation table, especially if you need to get something off your chest. Your community can handle it.

We can work it out—together.

The Coffee Table: When You Just Need a Break

Thankfully, there's a kind of table fellowship that's spontaneous, relaxing, unpretentious, and open to anyone at almost any time. It happens at the coffee table, and people from every group, team, family, corporation, school board, church, and civic organization need some time simply to hang out there.

The kitchen table functions best when people need a warm place to gather and some good food to share. The conference table is the optimal environment for wrestling with decisions. The negotiation table requires emotional courage and intense focus. But the coffee table needs absolutely, positively nothing, except maybe coffee or tea!

And that's the point.

The coffee table has a placard on it that says, "Warning: You are entering a de-construction zone—please remove your hard hat!" It's safe, open, relaxed, and carefree. No pressure, no big agenda. Enter when you want, leave when you must.

When people need a casual, come-as-you-are, stay-as-long-as-you-want environment, they pull up a seat (or a couch, or a pillow, or a spot on the floor) at the coffee table. Drop by anytime, jump into the conversation anywhere, and slip out at any point. Or simply listen.

A young, recently married couple, Stephanie and Mike, showed up at a coffee table kind of gathering for people with tough questions about Jesus, the Christian faith, church, God's existence, and the spiritual life. He was virtually an atheist; she was a spiritually open person who had experimented with many religious and philosophical approaches to God and life. They occasionally dropped in at a local church and heard about a small gathering for people much like themselves. Upon arrival, they were pleased to find that most of the people were at various stages of truth seeking and had difficult, honest questions to ask. The gathering was informal and conversational, encouraged openness, and invited everyone to participate. And yes, there was coffee.

The facilitator who guided the loosely structured discussion time explained the only ground rule: all points of view were welcome, and since this was a church-sponsored gathering, the Christian perspective would always be one of them.

Perhaps because she was more spiritually open, or because she had ruled out many other approaches and philosophies in her wide-ranging religious experience, Stephanie was intrigued by the life of Jesus and found answers to many of her questions in the Bible (which she read on her own at home). Mike, however, seemed to have more questions than anyone could answer. He was neither belligerent nor combative, but simply stuck and uncertain. Nevertheless, he found the teachings and life of Jesus compelling.

Months after his wife became a believer, Mike jumped in. I remember asking what helped him to arrive at his conclusion. Interestingly, Mike's brother was a devoted Christian and had talked with him often about his questions. I remarked, "Surely that family relationship, combined with some clear answers, was a key factor in your coming to faith."

"Yes, that's true. He was always helpful with the explanations I needed. But that is not why I became a follower." At first I was a bit stunned. What a perfect situation—to have a brother who loves you, is patient in the process, and can answer your spiritual questions whenever you need to talk. "Actually, it was the discussion group. That's what sealed it." *The coffee table? Really? It was not even a Bible study group. How could such a loose gathering have such a decisive impact?*

"Like others in the room, I had my share of questions," he continued. "And I found many answers. But I confess I still have lots of questions today." *OK, now I am really confused. It was not your brother's answers. And you have more questions now than when you started. Yet you became a follower of Christ.* "Despite all the questions, there was one fact I could not debate or deny: the changed lives of people in the group. I closely watched the two Christians in our group. I watched carefully as others became followers. They had something I wanted. They were becoming the kinds of people I wanted to be like. And, of course, I could see my wife's growth on a daily basis. I became a Christian because of Christians."

OK, full disclosure on my part. I have heard people say they would *never* become a Christian because of what they had seen in Christians. It's sad, and too often it's true. I wish it were not so. Yet I have been hanging around Christians for over thirty years, and I must say that most of the time their lives provide a compelling reason to look at Jesus and consider his claims. I know because I too became a Christian primarily because of Christians.

Mike and Stephanie encountered Jesus at that coffee table. You can read that sentence two ways. They "encountered Jesus" while they were sitting at the table, or they actually met Jesus in the lives of Megan or Christy or Dr. Owens or Elizabeth, who showed up each week. They met Jesus in his followers.

We desperately need coffee table conversations and relationships. The coffee table is a perfect place to be because we can choose our favorite blend. Some like the lighter roast—the casual conversation blend—while others prefer a little sweetener like love or friendship to compensate for some bitterness. Others want it bold and strong, without compromise and full bodied so they can gulp down the raw truth about God and life just as it is.

So what will it be? An extra-grace venti? A double shot of kindness? The truth-teller special? Friendship blend?

Grab a mug. Put your feet up awhile. Relax. Let's talk.

The Seminar Table: When You're Searching for Answers

I'm a professor, consultant, public speaker, and seminar leader. I love teaching, and I thought I understood my craft pretty well until one day I read Parker Palmer's description of the art of teaching: "To teach is to create a space in which obedience to truth is practiced."[3]

It rocked my thinking and stirred my soul. That's exactly what I want my craft to be! Not simply information transfer or a constant content barrage. I want teaching that produces change. Perhaps this is why I was so attracted to Jesus's brand of teaching. He was creating a learning culture, not just building a teaching platform. He wanted listeners to engage with truth and practice it.

> Therefore everyone who hears these words of mine and puts them into practice is like a wise man who built his house on the rock. The rain came down, the streams rose, and the winds blew and beat against that house; yet it did not fall, because it had its foundation on the rock. But everyone who hears these words of mine and does not put them into practice is like a foolish man who built his house on sand. The rain came down, the streams rose, and the winds blew and beat against that house, and it fell with a great crash. (Matt. 7:24–27)

Jesus was arguably the greatest teacher ever to walk the planet. Yet he was interested in more than simply teaching. He wanted his students to be learners, and he never confused teaching with learning or talking with training. Listen to him again: "The student is not above the teacher, nor a servant above his master. It is enough for students to be like their teachers, and servants like their masters" (Matt. 10:24–25). Jesus does not say, "It is enough for the student to have the same *knowledge* as the teacher." Rather, he says that the student's goal is to become *like* the teacher. When we find a great teacher, we want to be like him or her. With research tools at our disposal, we might be able to gather the information the teacher has acquired, but to be *like* the teacher, to discern when and how to use that information in a way that transforms people and changes culture, takes many years.

Sharon Isbin is an amazing musician, but her rise to greatness was guided by many mentors and teachers, including some of the best in the world. It all began at age nine when Sharon took her brother to an interview for guitar lessons with a popular artist touring Italy, where her family had recently moved. When Sharon's brother discovered it was not the rock music style of Elvis Presley he would be studying but rather classical guitar, he was uninterested. Sharon decided to take his place and soon began to study with the best guitarists in Europe.

At age sixteen, she returned to her birthplace, Minneapolis, where she was initially on her own. So she pursued mentors like world-renowned Andrés Segovia, whom some consider the best of all time. She also spent five summers with Oscar Ghiglia at the Aspen Musical Festival. She listened to tapes (before the CD era) and spent ten years in school under Bach keyboard scholar Rosalyn Turek. It took decades to put her knowledge into practice. Today, the eager student has become like her teachers. She now has their wisdom, experience, maturity, and skills. She has embraced music as a way of life, an extension of herself that blesses audiences worldwide. Close your eyes sometime and listen to her play.

Information is essential, but alone it is inadequate for producing real change. Teaching and learning are intended to be communal experiences. That's why Palmer says that the purpose of education is not to control others and not to arouse curiosity. The purpose of education—and of knowledge, specifically—he asserts, is compassion.[4] We gather data and gain insight in order to serve the needs of others—not only to provide personal growth, medical help, food production, understanding, training, and peace but also to help the next generation succeed. We pursue knowledge because we care about the development of others, not simply our own agenda.

At times your table will become a seminar table, a place to grapple with big ideas, enlarge minds with new concepts, and wrestle with how to turn lively discussions into life principles. You'll become a learning community striving for both personal transformation and meaningful impact.

Think of the people, groups, and teams who surround you. Do they push you to become bolder, wiser, and stronger? Do you invest in their growth? Are you eager to become a learning community instead of simply a talking community? If so, the Teacher is ready. But don't expect to stay in the classroom; learning only begins there. Venture outside and put it into practice.

The Operating Table: When Your Soul Needs Surgery

In April 2007, I began to feel a deep, throbbing ache in my right shoulder. A few days of rest followed by a much lighter fitness workout provided no relief. The pain became so bad that I could not lift my arm higher than my shoulder. I decided to see an orthopedic specialist. After his examination and evaluation of the MRI results, he broke the news to me.

"You have a torn labrum, and therapy is not an option. If you want to use that arm again, you'll need surgery. You have a bucket handle tear." He could tell I was trying to envision the injury, so he added some details. "The labrum is like a thick, circular band around your shoulder joint, and it attaches to the bone. Yours is ripped apart and hanging off the shoulder joint like a bucket handle. We need to sew it back onto the shoulder." Take note, fitness freaks. Exercise is dangerous to your health!

I was only half listening. As he talked, I deleted lines from the wonderful script I had penned for my next twelve months . . . and beyond. Then he quipped, "And when I operate, if I find any more mess, like damage to the rotator cuff or soft tissues, I'll clean it up while I'm in there." He sounded like he was talking about clearing out his garage.

"How long will I be out of action?" I asked with obvious frustration. I had been anticipating summer camp with my daughter, travel abroad for work, and a full golf season. "You won't be able to do anything for a month, and you'll have to sleep in a recliner. Then you'll need therapy for probably six months. It depends." "It depends" is what a doctor says to avoid malpractice suits. He really means you have a 50-50 chance of ever combing your hair again, let alone playing catch with your kids. Four-year-olds will beat you at bowling. "And golf is probably out of the picture until next year," he added. "Unless all you do is putt." He smirked when he delivered that last line. So I punched him in the face with my good arm. Not really. But the thought crossed my carnal little mind.

Here's the plain truth. I absolutely needed that surgery. And I totally hated having that surgery. The more I could see the long-term benefit, however, the more I began to almost look forward to it. I wanted healing. I needed relief. Today I have about 95 percent mobility, I can work out (more carefully than before), and I play golf at exactly the same level (because nothing can make my game worse, not even shoulder surgery). There are some scars, and I will always have mild, intermittent pain. It's a small price to pay, especially compared to the medical bill.

So it is in the spiritual life. Great change often requires enduring deep suffering or discomfort. You and I are surrounded by people with deep wounds and emotional injuries that must be probed, named, and repaired with the scalpel of truth and the ointment of grace. There may be scars, pain, and trauma, but individuals and groups who care about long-term health are committed to doing what is needed to eradicate the toxic material in our systems and facilitate recovery.

Work at the operating table is usually done by close friends and respected experts (counselors, therapists, and pastors). It requires the insightful skills of others. Not even my doctor could perform surgery on himself. So why do we try? Why do we lie to ourselves, saying, "I can handle it"?

The truth is that you can't handle it. Not alone, at least. That's why you are stuck, frustrated, emotionally harmful to others, and angry about your own dismal progress. You have personal work to do, like the exercises I practiced during therapy and still do today. But it takes a community to run the operating room when it's your turn to lie on the table.

Caitlin was a beautiful, creative, nineteen-year-old college sophomore whose passion for art was matched only by her love for people. She could fill a room with her presence without making anyone feel small or insignificant. Her joy was irrepressible and contagious. I always felt better just talking with her. She had a glimmer in her eyes that made you smile but also hinted that she might be contemplating some mischievous deed at your expense. She was pure creative energy flowing into every life around her.

And then one day the glimmer was gone; the energy flowed no more.

While home for summer break, she was driving to her job when, for reasons unknown at the time, she swerved into oncoming traffic, striking another vehicle head-on. She was rushed to the emergency room with severe head trauma and a plethora of other injuries.

Dozens of sobbing students and friends filled the waiting room, praying, crying, wondering what had happened, numb from shock, and gripped with fear. Her father, formerly an ER doctor and now an associate pastor at the church where we both worked, remained in constant contact with hospital staff and physicians, giving us regular updates. Then the news we all dreaded arrived, spoken from his courageous but quivering lips: "The doctors have confirmed that she is brain dead, and there is nothing we can do to save her." Shrieks of agony and uncontrollable wailing filled the room as the family sank into the couch, overwhelmed by unimaginable horror. My body sagged as I clung to a nearby pillar and tried to comprehend the unbelievable.

Watching these dear friends of ours face the grim reality that their cherished daughter was suddenly gone was one of the most awful moments my wife and I have ever experienced. The following day she was removed from life support and pronounced dead.

Darkness filled the earth.

My friend, the ER doctor who had saved so many, along with his grief-stricken wife, now needed help to recover from a level of emotional and spiritual trauma that no parent should ever have to endure. I could not even begin to imagine the depth of their despair and pain. He and his wife would require months of time in the healing presence of the great Physician and the long-term efforts of "soul surgeons" working to bring hope and healing.

Soul surgeons in our lives are courageous and committed friends and professionals who ask the right questions, name the realities we must face, and help to prescribe the steps necessary for emotional and spiritual recovery to occur. The Holy Spirit comes alongside to guide and teach, and faithful pain partners pray, listen, mirror the truth back to us, celebrate our small steps, and cheer our big wins.

After the tragic death of their beloved daughter, my friends needed some soul surgery at the hands of skillful spiritual physicians followed by long-term care, rehab, and therapy. They are smart, competent, and dedicated followers of Christ, but they did not think for even a moment that they could recover from this heartbreak alone. They needed a community.

Don't let fear, self-sufficiency, or just plain foolish pride keep you from lying on the operating table. The pain will soon lessen, and the joy you long for will begin to emerge.

The Changing Table: When Life Gets Really Messy

Good friend and colleague Heather Zempel wrote a book titled *Community Is Messy*. It's worth every penny. Heather and I share the same view of life in community. Everything works really well—until people show up. Then it gets messy. If you want a spotless, sanitized life, just find a nice cell block in your favorite prison and ask them to put you in solitary confinement.

And good luck, because you'll discover you still have your own mess to deal with.

Stuff happens. There's a bumper sticker that says it more pungently, but this is a religious book, so "stuff" will suffice. You had better factor "mess" into every event you organize, every project you design, every group you join, and every vacation you plan. Mess is mandatory. Mess is woven into the fabric of life. As Heather exhorts, "When Jesus gave his last command, the Great Commission, he said, 'Go and make disciples of all nations.' He didn't say go *find* disciples. He said go *make* disciples. That means it's work. And that requires us to embrace and enter into the mess."[5]

In my coaching and consulting work, I help leaders to build authentic groups and teams, and I often use an exercise to help new groups have some fun as they get acquainted. I ask members to find something they have in common. I want them to explore their stories a bit and learn about one another. With multiple groups in the room, I set up a contest to see which team can discover a hidden commonality first. It can be fun and sometimes quite revealing.

Some discover they grew up in the same city or work in a similar profession. Others find they have the same number of kids or played the same sport in high school. At times a group discovers a common experience or trait that, while true, may not be considered attractive or funny. Sometimes people discover they share a common pain or trial, like members of a group who discovered they had all served time in prison. For others, it is a divorce, the loss of a loved one, an illness or life-threatening condition, or a debilitating surgery.

Community feels comfortable when we gather at the table of camaraderie. However, real friendships rarely form there. Problems remain hidden, and pain is generally ignored or repressed. Conversations hover at the cocktail party level, and relationships barely scratch the surface—until life happens and stories take dark turns. Moving into deeper community then requires real courage. The image of the changing table—especially for new parents—reminds us that the mess of life is not a distraction from real community but the catalyst for entering deeply into it. And (like in the case of a baby) the people who help you to clean up your mess are generally very close to you—or they become very intimate in the process.

The following examples from real groups and relationships pushed members to new levels of community, trust, and growth—but not before the mess had to be cleaned up.

My wife has been having an affair with a co-worker.

I was offered a new job at the company; it is an awful job. They obviously want me to resign and move on.

My aging parents have decided to commit suicide together in two weeks.

While we were on vacation, our former church publically announced we were being excommunicated because of sexual misconduct. It was a lie. We returned to find everyone against us. So now we are attending here. We need healing and hope to rebuild our ability to trust others.

I am a cutter. I hate myself. My high school friends ignore me.

Real communities create mess. Real communities work to clean it up. So put on your work clothes—it's messy out there.

Table Tales

I was one of the first to understand. Good or bad, news piques my interest, especially news about people who make a difference or overcome impossible odds. That's why I was one of the first disciples to follow Jesus. I was eagerly awaiting the Messiah long before he appeared. As a disciple of John the Baptist, who proclaimed himself to be "preparing the way" for the Messiah, I was ready.

Sitting here tonight, I wonder if these eleven understand the big picture. They're confused about the present, fearful of the future, and ignorant of the past. And that irritates me, especially about our past, our story. Peter, James, and John should know better because they spend the most time with him. Don't they see that the past is prologue for everything that is happening? Only

Jesus seems to be clued in, but even he seems more somber and heavyhearted tonight.

I remember seeing him by the sea, and when he said, "Come, follow me," I couldn't drop my net fast enough. Later, I brought my brother Simon to him, because there is only one thing better than hearing a good story, and that's reporting it. I told Simon, "I have found the Messiah!" Big brothers tend to ignore little brothers. But not this time. Oh, at first he was startled, wondering if I had spent too much time with the locust-and-honey-eating baptizer. When he saw I was serious, he and I raced to see Jesus. Jesus looked him straight in the eyes, said "You are Peter," and invited him to follow as well.

But here is where the story takes a bad turn, at least in my mind. I am still angry about it. I was first to see Jesus. I brought Simon Peter to meet Jesus. I studied with John the Baptizer and recognized our Rome-conquering Messiah right away. But soon Peter, James, and John became "the big three," as we call them. Whenever something really significant is going to happen, he takes the big three with him. Why not me? Too young? Too eager? Too smart? Too much in common with the camel-hair prophet? I have come to love Jesus, but I admit I am tired of hearing "Peter, James, and John . . . Peter, James, and John." Why choose my brother and not me? He chose James *and* John!

Just recently Jesus told us about the destruction of the temple and revealed signs about the end of all things. It was a little intimidating, but what a story. Now at Passover, I am excited but confused, waiting for the next big story. Whatever it is, I am going to make sure I have a front-row seat. Maybe, just maybe, Jesus will see me for who I really am. Then people will start talking about "the big four."

Now *that* will make a great story!

I am Andrew.

The Greatest Stories Ever Told

Everyone loves a great story—on the page, on the stage, or on the screen. But sometimes we fail to see the power of our *communal* story, shaped by our lives and shared in relationship. In a community, one grand narrative is unfolding, but the unfolding story has three substories that are woven together.

Each of these three stories needs to be understood and told or our table fellowship will be much shallower, less enriching, and not as satisfying to our souls. In fact, failure to tell any one of these stories may ruin the entire table experience.

The three stories are your story, God's story, and our story.

Your Story

After a speaking engagement in Nashville, I hailed a taxi and headed to the airport. My driver, Hassan (not his real name), eagerly explained why his service was the best, his fare most affordable, and his company more reliable than the competition. I smiled at his confidence and likability and then asked how long he'd lived in Nashville. "Since I was sixteen years old," he said thoughtfully. "I am a refugee," he confided, speaking in clear but sometimes broken English. "I fled Iraq in the 1990s. The Ba'ath Party was in control, under Saddam Hussein, and had drafted my father into military service to fight Iran.

"You see," he continued, "we are Shia, but the country was controlled by the minority Sunni under Hussein. It was

87

difficult, but my father served almost ten years. Then they wanted him to fight more, but he said, 'No, draft the younger men to fight for you, like you drafted me. I have served more than I am required.'" He glanced at me in his rearview mirror as his voice quieted and a deep sadness covered his face. "They came to our house three times to make my father enlist again, but he refused. The fourth time they shot and killed him. I was ten."

There are few words of consolation one can share in reply to a story like this. I could only say, "I am so sorry," but my words felt shallow. I asked what happened after that.

"When I was sixteen, a few of us fled to Saudi Arabia and then later to America. Before the 9/11 attacks at the World Trade Center, people welcomed me with open arms when they heard I was from Iraq. After 9/11, they just spit on me." I was so disgusted to hear this.

"How do they treat you now?" I asked.

"It is better. I now have some American friends, and I still love this country. I miss my home, and my mother is still there. I want to go back and visit. But at least I have friends here, and it is OK now."

When Hassan opened the door to his cab, he unlocked the door of his life and invited me to enter. His story served as the threshold. So does yours. Without your story, you are simply a random cache of data to the members of your community.

> He's six foot two, has brownish-gray hair, grew up on the East Coast, played some football in college, got married, has two kids, and sells computer software in Detroit.

She's young, single, and lives with her mother in a run-down apartment on the east side of Dallas, works two part-time jobs, has a three-year-old son, and drives a compact car.

So what? That's not a story. That's barely an outline; it's only bullet points on a page. We could try to patch a story together and fill in the many empty blanks along the way. But we'd likely be off base, passing unjust judgments and holding unwarranted assumptions.

People want to hear your story. They *need* to hear your story. Without your story, you do not have a relationship with the community. And without relationships, a community will never reach its potential.

Dan Allender quotes Hollywood screenwriter Robert McKee as he describes the art of storytelling:

> It begins with a situation in which life is relatively in balance: you come to work day after day, week after week, and everything's fine. You expect it will go on that way. But then there's an event—in screenwriting, we call it the "inciting incident"—that throws life out of balance. You get a new job, or the boss dies of a heart attack, or a big customer threatens to leave. The story goes on to describe how, in an effort to restore balance, the protagonist's subjective expectations crash. . . . A good storyteller describes what it's like to deal with these opposing forces, calling on the protagonist to dig deeper, work with scarce resources, make difficult decisions, take action despite risks, and ultimately discover the truth.[1]

Allender explains further that good stories describe the intersection of desire ("subjective expectation") and tragedy ("a cruel reality").[2] Hassan, my cab driver, had high hopes for himself and his family in the country of Iraq. But those hopes were dashed when a cruel and oppressive dictator ended the life of his father, killing him in cold blood. That tragedy shaped him and marked his life forever. From that point on, his story would never be the same.

What is your "subjective expectation"? What are your hopes and dreams and longings? If you could plot out your journey over the next few years, what would it look like? How would you express your deepest passion (your suffering, which is what *passion* means)? What kind of people would you meet? Where would you make your greatest impact? These questions and many others provide a framework for your imagined story. You are aware, I hope, that your hypothetical story will likely never come to pass. Life's "cruel realities" will intervene, forcing you to make dramatic turns or perhaps even a full turnabout.

Despite a reasonably good life for our family of four, in just the last ten years we have experienced the following: the death of three elderly parents, a shoulder surgery, two major car accidents (and some minor ones), a broken leg, two career changes, a four-month-long serious eye condition, several sports-related sprains, some financial challenges, and a dozen more "minor incidents" at school and work. In addition, our one remaining parent suffered a broken back, at least three head injuries from falls, and a number of ailments and illnesses.

Why would we think that the next five to ten years would be any different? What insanity do we embrace that tells us our lives will move ahead as planned? I look at some of my friends who have endured unspeakable losses and incessant pain, and I feel blessed by comparison.

So what can you do? You can make responsible plans for your future (seek wise financial guidance, medical advice, legal counsel), but remember that you cannot predict the outcome. You can honor how you are "wired" and leverage your gifts and talents. You can live in your values—truth, trust, grace, compassion, perseverance—even though you cannot predict what lies around the next bend of the journey. But you can also do something very powerful now. You can tell your life story up to this moment in time. From that story, you can mine precious jewels from your rocky past. You can do the honest, hard work of learning from (not living in) your mistakes, wrongdoings, and failures.

Here are some things to consider and some guidelines to follow as you prepare to tell your story at the table of community.

Less is more. Don't tell the whole story. As a friend of mine says, "There are Papa Bear stories, Baby Bear stories, and stories that are just right." It is often wise to start small. Not everyone needs to hear the full story. Consider telling the whole story—the Papa Bear version—to a close, trusted friend. By sharing a shorter version in community, you allow others the opportunity to ask questions about areas of the story that are intriguing or particularly meaningful.

Describe what you've learned, not simply what happened. We want to know how the experience you shared has shaped your life. "After that, I began to understand . . ." is a good way to frame it. It is sufficient to provide a brief overview highlighting the defining moments, and then you can add your key responses, decisions, emotions, and the impact on your life.

Don't compare your story with the stories of others. Too often we hear, "Oh, there's nothing exciting about my story." A member of your community shares a riveting, dark, traumatic, and powerfully redemptive story before you tell yours. You're serving oatmeal to a group that just finished the grand-slam breakfast at Denny's. Sure, God changes lives in dramatic fashion. These are "I was on my way to Damascus when I was blinded by a light" apostle Paul kind of stories.

Remember, however, that there are many Peter and John stories—stories of the "and they dropped their nets and followed him" variety. Nothing overly dramatic. No addictions, no marital meltdown, no prodigal-son lifestyles. Just a simple but transforming encounter with Jesus that may take years to unfold. Your story doesn't have to rock the room; it already shakes the heavens. That should be enough drama for anyone.[3]

Be real without being offensive. We love authenticity—to a point. Years ago, I attended a church where members shared responses to the message after the sermon. People shared valuable insights and noted Scripture passages they appreciated. It was generally an encouraging and productive time. Then a woman awkwardly shared intimate details about a very private surgery. Immediately, the TMI (too much information) indicator began flashing on the church etiquette dashboard. Many elderly women fainted. (Not surprisingly, elderly men increased the volume on their hearing aids and shifted to the front rows.) The leaders announced an end to sharing services "due to the unforeseen psychological trauma" they caused. No one complained. But on Monday, CD sales of the service broke a thirty-year record. You get the point.

Finish with today. The past is powerful, but tell us where you are now. We know about your story; now tell us the condition of your soul. What brokenness remains, what new insights are emerging, what is God saying to you now? Your story does not have to be neatly packaged and wrapped with a pretty bow. There can be loose ends, uncertainties, and some awkwardness about the present. Don't be afraid to share that, and don't shy away from your optimism about the future. Your optimism is what you have today, and people need to hear that. It's a beautiful part of you.

So tell us a story—your story. We're all listening.

God's Story

If all we had on this planet was your story and my story, we would be in deep weeds. Thank goodness there's a greater story guiding us, within which our stories are unique and captivating chapters. God's story began long before our stories and will continue to unfold after the final pages of our stories have been written. And that's good news—very good news! God's story is all about good news. Allow me to tell you his story so you can tell it to the people at your table. Though brief, this story is absolutely critical to participating in table fellowship with Jesus.[4]

In the beginning, before time as we know it, the Triune God—Father, Son, Spirit—created the heavens and the earth. As part of that beautiful and amazing creation, he made man and woman in his image to enjoy fellowship with him, care for and develop his creation, and multiply. From the beginning, God was building a community, a covenant people for himself who would enjoy and serve him, even as he would enjoy and serve them.

Being made in God's communal image was no small thing. Humans were created with hearts, minds, desires, and wills of their own—but also with the need to be in relationship with God and one another. However, the first humans were curious and chose to be *like* God instead of enjoying their relationship *with* God. They chose to go it alone, without God. As a result of that choice, four relationships were severed:

with themselves: a confident, joy-filled, serenity of soul was replaced with guilt and shame and fear in their hearts;

with one another: unbridled affection, unbroken relationship, and undivided purpose gave way to interpersonal conflict, physical pain, and a lust for power and control;

with the earth: the exhilaration that accompanies passionate creativity and endless productivity at work was crushed, replaced by agonizing toil and constant frustration;

with God: they experienced alienation from their Creator, whom they had disobeyed and ignored.

As a result, Adam and Eve were forced to leave Eden, but not before God gave them a promise, assuring them that the deceiver who had lured them away from him would someday be crushed and a way would be made for everything to be set right again. Their souls needed rescuing; their relationships, all four, needed restoration. This was something they could never achieve on their own. God would have to do it for them.

After bringing a planet-cleansing flood to eradicate evil and rescuing Noah's family, God began a new relationship with the human race. But God's people strayed from his ways again and again. God (who never gives up on his people) chose Abraham and his family to build a new community—a people for his possession through whom he would bless the entire world. Eventually, God led Abraham's grandson Jacob to Egypt to protect his family from a severe famine. But sadly, after the rise of a new pharaoh, Abraham's descendants would find themselves enslaved under cruel Egyptian oppressors for four hundred years.

Finally, a rescuer named Moses was chosen to set his people free, but this freedom came at a price. Lambs' blood was shed and painted on their doorposts so that death would pass over them, a graphic depiction of the atoning sacrifice needed to cleanse the sins of a community that had rebelled for so many years. Their rescue, the exodus, became the defining story of the Hebrews for generations to come and is memorialized in the Passover feast, which commemorates the saving work of God. He redeemed a people for his own possession.

After receiving God's holy laws for living the kingdom life, the Israelites entered the land that was promised to Abraham, Isaac, and Jacob. But their prosperity was short lived and so was their faith. They grumbled and complained and rebelled and whined about everything. For centuries, they repeated the same cycle that began in the garden paradise: turn from God, suffer the consequences, repent and return, and be rescued by a merciful God.

Eventually, the people clamored for a king like the nations around them, rejecting God as their King. After some disastrous leaders, a new king—David, a man after God's own heart—came to the throne of Israel. Despite his many failings and gross misconduct, he received yet another covenant from God to enact with his people. This one was the clearest yet, promising an anointed leader, a conquering king, a real Messiah!

Yet things moved from bad to worse and included rebellion, oppressive kings, overzealous prophets, wars, famine, idolatry, cruelty, and ultimately captivity at the hands of ruthless Babylon for seventy years. But once more God rescued his people; he returned them to Jerusalem in 538 BC, to the promised land Joshua had first conquered almost a thousand years earlier. The Israelites received a few more words from a few more prophets and then silence, for four hundred years.

The Jews waited anxiously for their conquering Messiah-Warrior. There were rumors of signs, and many looked for any indication of prophetic rumblings. Meanwhile, amid the prophetic silence, a poor young couple in the obscure village of Nazareth received angelic visitations. "You will bear a child, a son, a Savior for the world. His name will be Jesus" (see Luke 1:30–33; Matt. 1:20–21). Almost thirty years later, after serving in his father's carpentry business, Jesus launched his public ministry with the blessing of his heavenly Father and the baptism of John.

He taught the crowds, healed many, confronted religious elitism, loved all people, and then suffered at the hands of unrighteous men who put him to death on a cross, just as the prophets had predicted. This was his mission. No military coup, no political house cleaning, no religious power struggle. Just a cross. The temple curtain was rent in two, the earth shook, local graves gave up their dead, direct access to God was made available, and sin was atoned for as Christ breathed his last and said, "It is finished" (Matt. 27:50–53; John 19:30).

Three days later, resurrection power was unleashed, Jesus's tombstone was rolled away, and angels proclaimed, "He is not here; he has risen!" (Luke 24:6).

He is risen indeed!

But God's story doesn't end there.

Jesus spent seven weeks teaching his followers about life in the new community. He prepared them to be colaborers in the building of his church, the same church you and I serve in today. He ascended to the Father, leaving us the Holy Spirit to guide and empower our lives and ministry. The charge to "go and make disciples of all nations" (Matt. 28:19) is as relevant today as it was that day, as is his promise: "I am with you always, to the very end of the age" (Matt. 28:20).

In Jesus's name, we deploy the gifts he has given us to serve the world, strengthen his people, seek the lost, bind up the broken, heal the sick, and share the story with people in every corner of the earth. We labor until he comes again to set everything in the cosmos right, not just our relationship with God. All of creation will be renewed. All four relationships, broken at the beginning of the story, will be reconciled and made new. When he returns, everything will be far better than it was in the beginning—a new heaven and a new earth and new bodies. Can I get an amen? *Everything* will be made new.

That's the story. For those of you who drifted off to sleep, here's a recap:

At creation, the Triune Community was revealed.

In the garden, community was rejected.

At the cross, community was redeemed.

In the church, community has been recovered.

In the new creation, community will be restored.[5]

We find the image of the table, of communal life, present in every act of the drama, from the Trinity to eternity. It's all about community with God through Christ in us.

At the table, your story meets God's story so that we can write our story.

Our Story

Every family, group, church, and organization has a story. And so does yours. All your individual stories are woven together to produce a tightly knit garment of community, showing the world your strength and beauty.

In 2008, after my son's high school graduation, we traveled to Australia and New Zealand, where I was speaking for Willow Creek. No, it is not usual for me to provide an exotic, international trip for my children's graduations, but in this perfect storm, great timing, award travel, and free housing made the opportunity irresistible.

In Sydney, we decided to make the Harbour Bridge climb. Built in 1932 and rising about five hundred feet above sea level, the bridge offers a stunning panoramic view of Sydney. Between various sections of the bridge, you must travel across narrow walkways hundreds of feet above the ground, tethered to the walkway by cables hooked to a carabiner.

Despite a few mild concerns, the Harbour Bridge tour was a smashing success. Ryan did the climb on Wednesday while I did some reading, and then I went by myself on Thursday while he finished some shopping. It was great that each of us could do it by ourselves.

Are you kidding?

Of course we completed the climb together. Together is better because we have an experience to share that is different than two separate but equal experiences could ever be. Doing that climb with my son was a remarkable experience.

God's spirit performs a unifying work when we bring our stories together. That oneness— prayed for by Christ in John 17, revealed in the Trinity, practiced by Jesus and the Twelve, and essential to the life of the church—is mysterious and transformational. When we gather at the table and declare our oneness, we are making a statement that in community we have authority and power.

In his book *Better Together*, Robert Putnam explains how the power of community can get something done. He describes how a group of sixth graders in the town of Waupun, Wisconsin, joined forces to bring much-needed change.

Working with an organization called Do Something, these kids banded together with local authorities to redesign the safety system for a railroad crossing in the town. Here's the cool part. Do Something allowed the kids to design the project, build their own team, and work directly with local officials to get the job done. Though a national organization, Do Something did not use its "muscle" to bring about the needed changes—they empowered a small group of committed kids to solve a problem. Instead of being the result of a professional media campaign or a response to a series of isolated phone complaints from parents, the change came when a small group of kids, each with a story and a passion for safety, locked arms and got the job done.

Imagine the story those kids have. Imagine how they feel, having experienced this together. Now imagine your story as a group or a team. Imagine how your individual stories, your group story, and God's story all come together for life change and progress. A pastor friend of mine says, "Discipleship occurs when our story meets God's story to form a new story. The more our story looks like his story, the more we change and grow. It's that simple."

That is what a table can do. We come together in community and find our place and sense of welcome, unity, and deeper connection. We learn to do life together in our little circle and soon discover that table fellowship in the name of Jesus is not restricted to one expression of communal life or held captive by rigid routines or rules. It is flexible, creative, and dynamic. Our table may take different forms over time as our purpose changes or new members arrive with their stories. Soon new chapters are written and our story unfolds in ways we could never have imagined. Our table starts to look more like Jesus's table.

Now we are ready for something more—not just something we can *be* together but something we can *do* together.

It's time to pick up a towel.

PART 2

Practice the Ministry of the Towel

It was just before the Passover Festival. Jesus knew that the hour had come for him to leave this world and go to the Father. Having loved his own who were in the world, he loved them to the end.

The evening meal was in progress, and the devil had already prompted Judas, the son of Simon Iscariot, to betray Jesus. Jesus knew that the Father had put all things under his power and that he had come from God and was returning to God; so he got up from the meal, took off his outer clothing, and wrapped a towel around his waist. After that, he poured water into a basin and began to wash his disciples' feet, drying them with the towel that was wrapped around him.

He came to Simon Peter, who said to him, "Lord, are you going to wash my feet?"

Jesus replied, "You do not realize now what I'm doing, but later you will understand."

"No," said Peter, "you shall never wash my feet."

Jesus answered, "Unless I wash you, you have no part with me."

"Then, Lord," Simon Peter replied, "not just my feet but my hands and my head as well!"

Jesus answered, "Those who have had a bath need only to wash their feet; their whole body is clean. And you are clean, though not every one of you." For he knew who was going to betray him, and that was why he said not every one was clean.

When he had finished washing their feet, he put on his clothes and returned to his place. "Do you understand what I have done for you?" he asked them. "You call me 'Teacher' and 'Lord,' and rightly so, for that is what I am. Now that I, your Lord and Teacher, have washed your feet, you also should wash one another's feet. I have set you an example that you should do as I have done for you. Very truly I tell you, no servant is greater than his master, nor is a messenger greater than the one who sent him. Now that you know these things, you will be blessed if you do them." (John 13:1–17)

Why is it so difficult to pick up a towel? Are towels really that heavy? I must admit that sometimes it is so much easier to come to the table than to pick up a towel. I wish it were not so. But towels are some of the greatest community-building tools we will ever find at our disposal. Here is where the towel fits into an irresistible community.

> In community,
>> the table gives us meaning;
>>> the towel guides our mission,
>>>> the truth guards our message.

No one practiced the ministry of the towel better than Jesus. For Christ, serving was not simply an activity; it was his identity. Listen to the description of Jesus and the focus of his mission in Philippians 2:5–8:

> In your relationships with one another, have the same mindset as Christ Jesus:
>
>> Who, being in very nature God,
>>> did not consider equality with God something to be
>>>> used to his own advantage;
>> rather, he made himself nothing
>>> by taking the very nature of a servant,
>>> being made in human likeness.
>> And being found in appearance as a man,
>>> he humbled himself
>>> by becoming obedient to death—even death on a
>>>> cross!

At least three popular Bible translations of this passage read, "although"/"though" he existed in the form of God, he emptied himself, taking the form of a servant.[1] In other words, despite the fact that he was God, Jesus took on the form of a servant for a season here on earth so that he could humbly carry out his mission. Some scholars contend this is not the best translation because the Greek text simply says, "who being in the form of God" (v. 6); the word "although" is not present in the language. Then why translate it this way?

Because we assume that God is too high and mighty to be a servant by nature. He took the form of a servant, so it is logical to assume that prior to this point in time he was not a servant. Here's the truth: *because* God is so great and so mighty, he is a servant. Jesus took the form of a servant *because* he is God—and God at the core is a servant. So the idea is that Jesus, *because* he is by nature God, took the form of a servant. Biblical scholar Gerry Hawthorne convincingly argues that if you want to add a word to the text, *because* instead of *although* would be a better choice and more theologically accurate.[2]

Jesus took the form of a man because through the incarnation he became 100 percent human—he was a man. He was in the "form of God" (Phil. 2:6 NASB, ESV) because he *was* God. And he took on the "form" of a servant because he was—he *is*—a servant. It's his nature.

So Jesus has no problem picking up towels.

I was speaking at a conference, and during a break I found myself standing next to three women who were talking about their church. I was not trying to eavesdrop but could not help overhearing the conversation. "We were getting ready for the luncheon, preparing food and setting up the room for our congregational meeting, and our pastor just stood there while we all worked," one said with a wry smile. "He was just standing there sipping his coffee while we set up the chairs. I guess he doesn't do chairs," she quipped. They all laughed, but it was one of those funny-but-also-sad laughs, as if they expected he would act that way.

Jesus doesn't just do chairs. Jesus does feet. That's what servants do, and they don't worry about it. So come to the upper room because something amazing is happening—someone just grabbed a towel. And no one expected it.

But they should have. And so should we.

Your Towel Has a Name on It

I suppose I've always been a man of stark contrasts. My hands are calloused, but my heart is tender. I have great passion, but it's often crippled by overwhelming fear. I can be the first one in but the first one out. I want to be the leader, but I have a hard time following. I tend to overpromise but under-deliver. I'm impulsive, hard charging, and gutsy. One day I was so arrogant that I even rebuked Jesus to his face. It's embarrassing even to think about it. No wonder he called me "Satan." That really hurt, a punch in the gut, but I deserved it. No disciple had ever rebuked Jesus. And I did it not long after I had proudly declared, "You are the Messiah, the Son of the living God!" to the amazement of everyone.

Will I ever be able to change? Will he ever be satisfied with me? Could he ever really use me to build his church? Is there hope for me? I know he loves me. He did right from the beginning.

How can I forget the day he stood in my boat and preached to the crowds on the beach? I had great admiration for him but assumed he knew nothing about fishing. Who throws a net out in the heat of the midday sun? Jesus, that's who. I was a bundle of ignorance and arrogance. Yet he has been so patient with me. I know he has high expectations for me, but I fear I will never be the "rock" he hopes I will become.

Here I sit and wonder where all this is going. Part of me wishes I wasn't chosen to be the leader of this group, and the other part of me swells with pride. How will we ever become a winning team with me at the helm?

It's all crazy. I am unreliable, the group is unreasonable, and Jesus is unpredictable. Just a few minutes ago he washed my feet. It was the most awkward and amazing experience I have ever had. Wow, did I miss the point! The towel and the pitcher of water were just sitting there. Not a servant in sight. I should have been the first to take action—that's what leaders do. Instead, he stood up as if it were the most natural thing to do. Immediately, my reluctance turned to exuberance (that's me, from hot to cold to hot again).

I am going to change. I can do it. It's time to stop wavering. I am ready for action, no matter what lies ahead. I will never deny him. I will always defend him. Some day the others will look up to me instead of down at me. Especially my little brother, Andrew.

I will be strong. I am the rock. You can count on me.

I am Peter.

Anyone Seen My Towel?

If you've been to a number of hotels, you know that some hotels put their name on their towels. And some people have their bath towels monogrammed. We don't need monogrammed towels in our home, because we have plenty of hotel towels (just kidding). But it is interesting how a towel can communicate a sense of belonging and identity.

When people are baptized at our church, we provide towels. We practice immersion baptism, so people get wet from head to toe. It's nice to have a towel to dry off with after the ceremony, but these aren't just any towels. These towels have a name on them—the name of our church. A kind and generous member donates the towels every time we have a baptism. Since we have quite a large congregation, we hand out a lot of towels. They signify that the people who have been baptized have a new identity. The baptism itself declares their identity with Christ—with his death, burial, and resurrection, and with his global church. The towels we give them signify they are part of a local community, a fellowship of servants who love Jesus and walk in his ways. They are a part of the body of Christ (1 Cor. 12:13) and have declared their commitment to a community of his followers, a local church.

As you become part of a thriving community and pick up your towel, you discover it has a name on it as well. You might think it's your towel. But if you look more closely, you see that the initials woven into the fabric are "J. C." The monogram on your towel belongs to Jesus Christ because you serve in his name.

In early March 2006, my family and I traveled to Hawaii so I could speak at a church conference in Honolulu. After the three-day Honolulu conference, we spent a week on Maui to relax. *Maui* in Hawaiian means "Come to me all ye who labor and I will give you a condo on the beach." Or something close to that. It was going to be great!

Here's the bad news. The year 2006 was one of the worst in

Hawaii's history for rainfall. It poured heavily for fifty days. No typical midday showers you get accustomed to in the tropics. We saw the sun only two days out of ten. Honolulu experienced such great flooding that our hotel closed after a broken sewer line filled the street with waste. Thankfully, we had just departed for Maui. We figured that if we had to endure rain in March, Maui was the place to do it.

Despite escaping the floodwaters of Honolulu, we were ambushed by an even greater water disaster four thousand miles away. Men working outside our home washed their tools using an outdoor water spigot before leaving. Unfortunately, the water pipe leading from inside the home to that spigot had a crack in it. When they turned off the nozzle, the water continued to flow inside the home, flooding our finished basement.

Our house sitter, Susan, had no idea, because she had no reason to enter the basement. Thankfully, someone walked down there on day two of our trip and discovered the rising water. The 4:00 a.m. insurance call was one I will never forget. "This is State Farm, and we have a question about the water damage to your home." *Excuse me? Who?* Our gracious house sitter had urged them not to disturb us, but someone at the company had not gotten the message. We sure did.

Susan assured us that everything was OK and that water removal was under way. The insurance claim was filed, and our neighborhood was working feverishly to remove furniture and boxes from the wet basement. We struggled to enjoy our last days on Maui, including two days of sunshine but could only imagine what our basement looked like. Before returning home, Susan sent us an email.

Bill, don't worry—everything is OK. I am sorry you had to hear about all of this while you were on vacation. I tried my best. We can handle the details when you return. But I thought this might encourage you. Kevin, from the water removal company, has been here at least three times—moving fans around, cutting out damaged drywall, and checking on the progress of drying out the basement. Each time he seemed surprised to see people from the neighborhood working here. During his final visit he spoke with bewilderment. "Now let me get this straight. The family is in Hawaii, correct? And all these people coming in and out for three days are mostly neighbors, right?" "Yes," I told him, "that's correct." With a perplexed look on his face he asked—and you will love this—"Exactly what kind of neighborhood IS this?!"

What a great question! I had a few minutes to tell him more about the neighborhood small group and what you do. But I will never forget the look on his face. Indeed, what kind of neighborhood is this? What kind of community is this? He was seeing the body of Christ in action, and he was totally overwhelmed by it. Amazing.

We'll talk later. Fly safe. See you tomorrow.

The question reminded me of the Roman emperor Julian, who expressed a similar incredulity in the early centuries of the church: "The impious Galileans support not only their poor, but ours as well, everyone can see that our people lack aid from us."[1] In effect, "What kind of people are these?"

What kind of community do you have? What kind of church do people see when they look at your church? Rodney Clapp claims we are "a peculiar people," referring to heroic Old Testament believers who understood themselves as aliens and strangers in this world (Heb. 11:13–16, 39).[2] They lived a countercultural life for God by faith, even in the midst of great trials and despite never realizing the fulfillment of the messianic promises prophesied long before the birth of Jesus, whom they would never see.

An Identity Crisis

A serving community is a peculiar community, and that is sad. We are not often recognized or known for our service. Some Christians call themselves "people of the Book." But that would be wrong. Our friends in the Muslim community and many Orthodox Jews might refer to themselves as people of the Book. True, we have a book, and it is the greatest book ever compiled, coauthored by over forty people along with the Holy Spirit (2 Pet. 1:20–21). But even our book does not call us "people of the Book." It does call us something else, a phrase used at least five times in the book of Acts (9:2; 19:9, 23; 24:14, 22). We are known as people of the Way.

That's correct—not people of the doctrinal statement, not people of the political party, not people of the latest trend. People of the Way. Difference makers whose unbridled love and unselfish lifestyle created a commotion everywhere they went. Many were attracted to this irresistible community; others hated its beauty and goodness. As a result, the people of the Way were "publically maligned" and caused a "disturbance" among idol manufacturers and were taken "as prisoners" by Saul of Tarsus (Acts 9:2; 19:9, 23). They served others and lived such Christlike lives that political power brokers and religious elites hated them. People of the Way did not protest on street corners, shut down government buildings, or sling mud at political candidates. They simply lived in the way of Jesus. Their identity was unmistakable.

Not so today. We have an identity crisis. Could it be that we have become people who are *in* the way rather than people *of* the Way? Are we more of a hindrance than a help to those with spiritual questions and interest in the Christian faith?

Before we think about confronting the culture, we better look in the mirror. Let's demonstrate that we are truly interested in change, that we actually care about people, and that we are willing to listen, especially to those who disagree with us. I am concerned that today we are more interested in being right than being righteous, more focused on winning seats on the court than making room at the table, more consumed with national morality than personal integrity.

To become people of the Way, we must become stewards of the towel—Jesus's towel. That means we need clarity about who we are as servants.

The late Brennan Manning offers a bold challenge to be the church of Jesus once again. His gritty words and passion call us to greater discipleship and an unflinching faith:

> Christian piety has trivialized the passionate God of Golgotha. Christian art has turned the unspeakable outrage of Calvary into dignified jewelry. Christian worship has sentimentalized monstrous scandal into sacred pageant. Organized religion has domesticated the crucified Lord of glory, turned him into a tame symbol.

In his landmark work *The Crucified God*, Jürgen Moltmann writes: "We have made the bitterness of the cross, the revelation of God in the cross of Jesus Christ, tolerable to ourselves by learning to understand it as a theological necessity for the process of salvation. As a result the cross loses its arbitrary and incomprehensible character." Of course, theological necessities do not sweat blood in the night.[3]

At the center of our faith story is a cross, and the towel is a partial extension of the meaning of that cross (though far easier to carry). Both capture the sacrificial service that should characterize followers of Jesus, the Suffering Servant described in Isaiah's extended song,[4] which begins in Isaiah 42:

> Here is my servant, whom I uphold,
>> my chosen one in whom I delight;
> I will put my Spirit on him,
>> and he will bring justice to the nations. (42:1)

The song finishes in chapter 53:

> He was despised and rejected by mankind,
>> a man of suffering, and familiar with pain.
> Like one from whom people hide their faces
>> he was despised, and we held him in low esteem.
> Surely he took up our pain
>> and bore our suffering,
> yet we considered him punished by God,
>> stricken by him, and afflicted.
> But he was pierced for our transgressions,
>> he was crushed for our iniquities;
> the punishment that brought us peace was on him,
>> and by his wounds we are healed.
> We all, like sheep, have gone astray,
>> each of us has turned to our own way;
> and the LORD has laid on him
>> the iniquity of us all. (53:3–6)

When we read the rest of chapter 53, we discover that it was the Father's will to "crush him and cause him to suffer" for our salvation (v. 10). This was the ultimate expression of love and service. Christ laid down his life for us, and we should be prepared to lay ours down for him and for one another. Doing so is the most all-encompassing expression of love for others and thus for Christ (John 15:13).

The cross of Christ is the central image and ultimate expression of divine servanthood; it reminds us of our core identity. Once we become committed to taking up a cross, picking up our towel is easy by comparison. When you and I choose to die to self, we are free to live for others. We don't neglect the self. We don't abuse the self, and we don't ignore the needs of the self. Instead, we put to death the old self—the self-indulgent, self-centered, self-righteous person who wants to conquer our flesh, control our future. Then we put on the new self—the self that Jesus, by his Spirit, is transforming—and we become the servant people we are destined to be: "Then he said to them all: 'Whoever wants to be my disciple must deny themselves and take up their cross daily and follow me. For whoever wants to save their life will lose it, but whoever loses their life for me will save it'" (Luke 9:23–24).

If we are willing to return to the cross and reclaim our identity as sacrificial servants (not something I claim to have mastered), we will be prepared to rightly engage the world with love, grace, and truth and even to lay down our lives for others. That, according to Jesus, is the ultimate expression of love.

Karen Wessel made such a sacrifice. CBS Chicago reporter Brad Edwards describes the ordeal:

A northwest suburban mom gave her life to save a 9-year-old child from drowning earlier this week.

Karen Wessel of Arlington Heights, 47, died after she went after the child in Star Lake, Wisc., on Tuesday.

It happened at a family getaway. Janice Potocki, Wessel's sister, says three children who had been playing on a sandbar got too far out in the water and had to be rescued.

Potocki says she got two children back safely but the third, who did not know how to swim, struggled with her. She became disoriented and almost drowned before Wessel jumped in to help.

Her sister likewise had a hard time bringing the youngster to safety.

"He was trying to crawl up her to get air, and he pushed her under too many times," [said] Potocki. . . . By the time they [got] her out of the water, her heart had already stopped once."

Efforts to revive Wessel did not succeed, she said, and she was pronounced dead an hour later after her organs failed.

The 9-year-old boy she saved reportedly is doing fine.[5]

It seems that those who put their lives at risk for others simply act in the moment without extended thought or consideration. Maybe they have picked up the servant's towel so many times that it is just second nature to act—regardless of the potential consequences. They are not deterred by the risks and spend little time wondering about what should be done. In the moment when action is needed, they are unconcerned with outward appearances or the opinions of others. They put their reputations on the line with no thought that "the water might be cold" or "this might mess up my hair" or "what will my friends think?" or even "I might look foolish." They just pick up a towel and serve.

That is our calling. Just pick it up and get to work.

But before we consider how to use the towel Jesus has provided, one more issue needs to be set straight—mission clarity. Celebrating our "servant center," which is rooted in the sacrificial love of Christ at the cross, carries us far along the path toward becoming full-fledged people of the Way—the way of the towel. Finally, we know who we are. But now we have to ask, "What are we going to do together?"

Mission Confusion

Confusion concerning the purpose of the church runs rampant today, at least in the United States. We remain fuzzy in our thinking despite God's clear direction on the matter. While there may be several key passages affirming our mission in the world, those that follow are some of the clearest and most widely known.

Jesus was clear about *his* mission.

> He went to Nazareth, where he had been brought up, and on the Sabbath day he went into the synagogue, as was his custom. He stood up to read, and the scroll of the prophet Isaiah was handed to him. Unrolling it, he found the place where it is written:
>
> > "The Spirit of the Lord is on me,
> >   because he has anointed me
> >   to proclaim good news to the poor.
> > He has sent me to proclaim freedom for the prisoners
> >   and recovery of sight for the blind,
> > to set the oppressed free,
> >   to proclaim the year of the Lord's favor."

Then he rolled up the scroll, gave it back to the attendant and sat down. The eyes of everyone in the synagogue were fastened on him. He began by saying to them, "Today this scripture is fulfilled in your hearing." (Luke 4:16–21)

For the Son of Man came to seek and to save the lost. (Luke 19:10)

Jesus was clear about *our* mission.

Then Jesus came to them and said, "All authority in heaven and on earth has been given to me. Therefore go and make disciples of all nations, baptizing them in the name of the Father and of the Son and of the Holy Spirit, and teaching them to obey everything I have commanded you. And surely I am with you always, to the very end of the age." (Matt. 28:18–20)

But you will receive power when the Holy Spirit comes on you; and you will be my witnesses in Jerusalem, and in all Judea and Samaria, and to the ends of the earth. (Acts 1:8)

As a community of Christ followers, we are called to go into the entire world and pursue the mission Jesus gave us, the one he modeled here on earth. We practice and share the good news about him and his work (the gospel) as we move into every arena of life.

Or, using the framework of this book, I'd say it this way:

We welcome one another to the fellowship of the table.

We serve one another with the ministry of the towel.

We guide one another in the practice of the truth.

It's just not that difficult to understand. So why the confusion?

The confusion arises because we get distracted. We begin a slow but destructive decline, slipping and sliding off course. Maybe we don't spend enough time at the table building community. Perhaps we refuse to pick up our towel to clarify our call to service in the kingdom, or we ignore the great treasure found in God's truth and lose our compass heading.

Here are some practical reasons why the mission gets neglected.

Too much time in *church leaves less time to* be *the church.* Meetings, socials, events, classes, meetings (did I say meetings?) are sapping our energy. Too much of a good thing is not a good thing. No boundaries mean no life, no relationships, no salt and no light in the world. So pay attention to how many church obligations and other activities are on your plate.

Frantic activity has replaced fruitful ministry. We are filling up our calendars but emptying our souls. Ignorant of our unique gifts, experiences, talents, and schedules, we trade fruitful impact for frenzied activity. If you want long-term ministry effectiveness, discover your unique contribution and focus your energy there (see 1 Tim. 4:12–16).

We have settled for more Bible study and less Bible practice. Head knowledge and content overload are poor substitutes for real learning. Learning Bible principles without putting them into practice produces Pharisees, not followers (see Matt. 7:24–27). Be sure to pause as you read and study and take classes. Ask yourself, "How will I put this truth into action this week?"

We have recruited people to our ministry rather than empowering theirs. The purpose of pastors and teachers and group leaders is to equip the body for ministry. When we leaders enlist church members to help us accomplish our ministry responsibilities (some of which are needed and legitimate), we may fail to equip them for the purpose God has gifted them to fulfill. Instead of being doers of ministry, staff are called to be trainers of ministers (see Eph. 4:11–13).

We have focused on filling seats rather than forming circles. Weekend services and strategic events are crucial to the life of the church, but the energy devoted to filling rows on the weekend must be balanced by the energy allotted to forming circles throughout the week. Worship services and key events create momentum. Life groups, ministry teams, missional communities, support and recovery groups, and prayer teams develop people. We must do both—draw audiences and make disciples.

Mission Clarity

What about your community? Is it on a mission? And what about you? Is your personal life on a mission? When a group of humble servants gathers to achieve a kingdom mission, the impact on the world is profound. Jean Vanier describes why this must be our focus:

> A community becomes truly and radiantly one when all its members have a sense of urgency in their mission. There are too many people in the world who have no hope. There are too many cries which go unheard. There are too many people dying in loneliness. It is when the members of a community realise that they are not there simply for themselves or their own sanctification, but to welcome the gift of God, to hasten his Kingdom and to quench the thirst in parched hearts through their prayer and sacrifice,

love and acts of service, that they will truly live community. A community is called to be a light in a world of darkness, a spring of fresh water in the Church and for all people. If a community becomes lukewarm, people will die of thirst. If it bears no fruit, the poor will die of hunger.[6]

The mission is service in the name of Jesus, sharing his Good News in word and deed. I fear our deeds are lagging behind the energy we place on words. We are a society increasingly characterized by information inundation. Words are cheap and easy; work requires effort and is difficult. And there is so much work to do. As Christ followers, service is not simply what we do; it is who we are.

Be the church.

Be the mission.

Grab your towel.

A Dirty Towel Is a Happy Towel

I feel a little claustrophobic in this upper room. Give me the open sea any day of the week. Since we put the fishing business aside, I confess I miss those late nights and early mornings on the water: the moonlight shimmering on the lake, cool breezes, and countless stars. I picture Father Abraham looking up at the same sky when God told him his descendants would outnumber the stars. I totally understand why his jaw dropped.

For years I spent the better portion of every day catching, cleaning, and selling fish. The rest of the day I spent mending, cleaning, and buying nets. Fish and nets. My friends could smell me long before they could see me. Not a glamorous line of work, but it paid the bills, and we always had some left over. My dad started the business, and we'd done fairly well. Sure, it meant long hours and short tempers. But it was worth it. Hard to believe that was three years ago. Now, thanks to Jesus, we're catching people—more exciting but far less profitable!

The way I figure it I'm number two in the pecking order here, despite multiple efforts to oust Peter. John and I made an attempt to secure the best seats at the table. Why not? We are movers and shakers, keen businesspeople, not timid like Bartholomew or crazy like Simon or sneaky like Judas Iscariot. And we have more energy than the rest of the group put together, except Peter, who can't decide which side of the fence he's on. But the plan to grab the number one and number two chairs backfired, and now everyone hates us. Boy, were they angry.

Every time I look across at Jesus I think of that day at the shoreline. John and I were cleaning our nets when he just walked up and asked us to follow him. We just about lost it! I still laugh when I think about our reaction. Most rabbis wouldn't give us the time of day. We've got a reputation for being a bit aggressive, having as much fun rocking the boat as we do sailing it.

But I think Jesus saw us as a ministry challenge and chose us as entertainment for the rest of the disciples. Soon he was calling us "sons of thunder." Most people knew me as "the greater," but I admit the "sons of thunder" label is even better. My brother and I like kicking up dust and hate business as usual. We make a lot of noise but not many friends. We tend to take over any group, fill any room.

I like hard work. This ministry role is harder than I thought, but I like the challenge. Something tells me that after tonight it's really going to be tense. We'll probably lose a few of the weaker players—Nathaniel, Thomas, Philip. Rumors are floating around that following Jesus any further might cost us our lives. I have lost some sleep over that. But if the time comes and the cause matters,

I hope I can muster the courage. Looks like I might have to step up my game. But I'm ready. I'm one of the "sons of thunder"!

I am James, son of Zebedee.

Towels Get Dirty

Picking up a towel can stifle your ego. Using it can stiffen your back. But that's the point. Towels are meant to be used. Clean towels serve as quaint decorations for upscale hotel rooms and store displays, but good luck finding one at your local mechanic's shop. A used towel is a dirty towel, and restoring one to its original grandeur is all but impossible. The towel Jesus wrapped around his waist was not the hotel variety; it was stained and tattered, worn and torn from household servants using it to swab thousands of feet.

Ministry is messy, and towels get dirty.

Our kids have served on a number of initiatives to help struggling, under-resourced families in places like Chicago, the Dominican Republic, Costa Rica, South Africa, and Guatemala. While they are away, we parents eagerly await updates about the progress being made, projects they are working on, and people they are meeting. One part of the experience remains constant: it is always a mess. The photos reveal sweaty faces and mud-soaked clothes, evidence of hard work performed in challenging circumstances.

But the contrasts are what move my heart and penetrate my soul. Amid the grit and grime there are smiles and songs, games and giggles. An orphaned child whose parents were ravaged by AIDS is hugged and tickled. Surrounded by suffering and despair, our kids hand out meals to smiling faces, give and receive love, swap stories and swab floors, wash dirty clothes and wipe runny noses. All in the name of Jesus. They serve and are served. They receive the gift of community even as they share it freely.

Just as there are many kinds of tables that characterize the inner workings of a community, there are varieties of towels for many forms of ministry. If you use your towel correctly—the way Jesus used it, the way James of Zebedee did—it will soon be worn and tattered from cleaning up the messes in people's lives. If you like to "get in there and mix it up" in ministry, if you're one of those "sons of thunder" or "daring daughters," you'll go through a pile of towels before the year is out.

Towels do not come with an owner's manual, but they should come with a label that tells us how and when to use them. I know; you'd think it would be obvious. "Grab towel. Rub against dirty surface. Repeat until clean. Put towel in laundry." But you'd be wrong. There are rules. Let's review some dos and don'ts concerning the ministry of the towel.

The Ministry of the Towel: Dos

Serve Inside and Outside Your Community

When we think of serving others, some of us look exclusively outside our community while others look only inward. We need to pay attention to both. Serving inside the circle means caring for the members of our group as we gather at the table. Knowing one another's skills and experiences helps us to bring not only our prayers and encouragement to others but also our expertise for solving problems and meeting needs.

There are two primary ways to serve outside our community. The first is to serve as individuals. Each of us serves independently, sharing our insights and experiences with the group. In this way, we are exposed to the varieties of needs and projects in our world. Hearing the stories of others encourages us to pursue new areas where we can use our gifts and express our compassion.

We can also serve as a group. Though it's challenging to coordinate calendars, gathering at least a few people to serve together outside the group is always a life-changing experience. There is power in community. Serving as a group generates a common experience that can help to build deeper relationships and a sense of purpose and meaning. When we work together outside the community, we learn skills that can be applied inside the community. While serving others, we learn to listen more intently, discover new gifts, sharpen existing abilities, and gain a sense of personal confidence that allows us to share more boldly inside the group.

Rescue the Poor, Orphan, Widow, and Stranger

Brennan Manning writes:

> To listen carefully to Jesus' words—"Be compassionate as your heavenly Father is compassionate" (Luke 6:36)—is to draw close to the Jesus of the gospels. Matthew's version reads, "You must therefore be perfect as your heavenly Father is perfect" (5:48). . . . Scripture scholars tell us that the two words (*compassionate* and *perfect*) can be reduced to the same reality. Donald Senior asserts that "following Jesus in his ministry of compassion defines the meaning of being perfect as your heavenly Father is perfect."[1]

Manning continues with a quote from Marcus Borg:

It is striking that "Be compassionate as God is compassionate" so closely echoes "Be holy as God is holy," even as it makes a radical substitution. The close parallel suggests that Jesus replaced the core value of purity with compassion. Compassion, not holiness, is the dominant quality of God, and is therefore to be the ethos of the community that mirrors God.[2]

The four groups in the Bible deserving the most compassion are the poor, the orphan, the widow, and the stranger. The first letters of these four words form an acronym—POWS. That's how I often think of them, as "prisoners of war" to the culture and to the circumstances that surround them. Who will help end their captivity?

Scripture is clear regarding the focus of our compassion. James 1:27 is a prime example: "Religion that God our Father accepts as pure and faultless is this: to look after orphans and widows in their distress and to keep oneself from being polluted by the world." Interestingly, James captures the sentiments expressed earlier. The parallel commands "be holy" and "be compassionate" are both woven into James 1:27. Manning completes the thought: "In any society, secular or sacred, where the haves don't share with the have-nots, the Kingdom of Satan reigns."[3] Indeed, this is why you and I should be willing, like James, son of Zebedee, to get our hands—and towels—dirty.

Observe Where the Spirit Is at Work

As we carry out works of service, it is logical for us to be focused on the task. And it's just as important to connect with the people in our midst. However, even as we do, we are apt to get caught up in all the activity and relationships and fail to ask what the Holy Spirit is doing. Here are some questions to ponder as we perform the ministry at hand.

What kind of mood is filling this place? Is it characterized by joy, sorrow, fear, frustration, celebration, or weariness, or is there simply a heavy, dark cloud hovering over the entire gathering? My family and I have served in some very dark places in the world. Some felt oppressive and sad while others, much to our surprise, had an air of peace and the presence of a tender joy despite harsh circumstances. As we observe the mood, we become more attentive to what the Spirit may be asking us to do.

What does the physical environment tell me? As we look around the room, across the field, or down the streets where we serve, what do we see? In what condition are the buildings? How are they cared for, if they are cared for at all? In what kind of spaces do these people live, work, and worship? Environments create a culture. The culture at a bar is much different from the culture in a classroom. The furnishings, the presence of windows, the use of color, the quality of the materials, and the money that was spent all communicate values and realities that often go unspoken. For example, a pastor friend of mine entered a large church facility worth tens of millions of dollars and asked, "How can a spirit of humility thrive here? Look around. Everything communicates pride, self-sufficiency, technological dependency, and comfort. It must be difficult to foster a humble, servant-oriented community in surroundings like these." He was not being judgmental, just observant. I believe his question came from the heart, and the Spirit used it to illustrate different ways church leaders utilize precious financial resources for ministry.

What is happening on the team? I like to observe team members when we are working on a project together. One team I served on had the privilege of serving outside Johannesburg, South Africa, in a small settlement of four thousand people. The typical twelve-by-fourteen-foot "home" was a small shack built with corrugated metal, wood, and plastic that rested on a dirt floor covered with old rugs. Our team consisted of local volunteers, my family, and a couple of people from an international mission agency. I was impressed with the loving spirit of local workers, the commitment of the young, single woman from the mission, and the compassion expressed by my children.

But we also noticed a spirit of weariness and discouragement in the heart of this young mission worker. My wife and I spent some time with her, praying and listening to her story. Two years in these oppressive conditions had clearly worn her down. She had seen little progress, felt very alone, and witnessed much misery. Our compassion warmed her heart and lifted her spirits, at least for a season.

Make Time for Making Friends

We might discover that some of our best friendships form in a serving environment. We have the opportunity to rub shoulders with others, seeing them at their best and at their worst. Serving together provides a new window into a person's life through which we can view their heart, attitude, giftedness, emotional stability, and sense of humor. As we find common ground, we build close friendships.

Recently, I took a group of graduate students to serve at a local book bank as part of a class I was teaching on building community in the church. I wanted them to experience the relationship-building power of service, especially since they barely knew each other. At the book bank, we sorted and packaged sets of donated books to be distributed to impoverished families in the Chicago area.

I watched as we worked in two teams. What began as a job turned into an opportunity to tell stories and share memories. As these twentysomethings and I completed a "quality inspection" on each book, we recognized titles and stories. Soon laughter and smiles filled the work space as students described early childhood experiences with their parents, places they had lived, and the family environment in which they had been raised. One student and I began to talk about our own kids, and he revealed serious dietary challenges faced by one of his young daughters. He was tender and thoughtful as he described her needs. I could tell he was a great dad—caring, strong, willing to do whatever it took for his kids. I felt a bond we would have likely never experienced in a typical classroom setting.

When I reflect further on my own experience, I can see that I built many friendships while doing ministry with others. But you have to be intentional. During breaks, shake some hands and introduce yourself. Set time aside for lunch, prayer, and reviewing the events of each day.

Pay Attention to What God Is Doing in Your Heart

The Spirit clearly works in teams. But he also does great work in individual hearts, so be willing to take a few moments to listen and observe. A close friend of mine joined a group of men on a work team serving in the Dominican Republic. At the time, he was a fence sitter. He attended weekend services and had done a little Bible reading, but he seemed to be hovering around the Christian faith without making a commitment to Christ. He describes what took place during the mission trip: "As I listened each night to these guys and I saw how they worked in the attitudes they expressed among the people, I became convinced that it was time to commit my life to Christ. I had a chance to see Christianity up close and personal. And it was real."

The next time you are serving others, pray a bold prayer. Ask the Holy Spirit to reveal the true nature of your own heart as you accomplish the task. Perhaps he will ask you some questions like these: Are you serving out of a sense of pride? Do you look down on those who appear to be lower on the ladder of life? Are you easily annoyed when things don't go exactly as planned? Must you always be the leader of the team? Do you avoid leadership and resent taking responsibility for the ministry? Do you find your love for others growing as you serve, or is a subtle bitterness beginning to develop? Do you resent the people or the situation around you?

Or perhaps you feel your heart getting softer. You find a greater sense of compassion growing within you, a longing to be merciful to those who desperately need mercy. Does this cause you to view your life, your possessions, and how you spend your time differently? Instead of simply serving these people, could you ever see yourself as one of their friends? Will they remain an object of your service, or might they become, by God's grace, the object of your affections?

These are difficult questions. The Holy Spirit uses these, and many like them, to intentionally and tenderly reshape your heart. So pay attention. There is so much to learn.

Remember That the Task Is the Tool for Spiritual Growth

Maybe you've had this experience: You show up to paint someone's home or help renovate an elementary school in a poor area of the city; or perhaps you spend a day serving at a homeless shelter expecting to help others with their problems and needs. But you soon realize that while you are doing ministry for others, the Spirit of God is doing a work in you. You're aware that you are receiving far more than you are giving. You may find that the people you are serving are serving you. These are some of the most powerful moments of spiritual growth that you will experience.

Too many of us believe that the only time we experience spiritual growth is during "spiritual activities" like praying, worshiping at a church service, or reading the Bible. While these will help to catalyze your growth, they are insufficient by themselves to produce spiritual maturity. Without service, your growth will be stunted.

James 1:22–25 drives the point home brilliantly and forcefully:

Do not merely listen to the word, and so deceive yourselves. Do what it says. Anyone who listens to the word but does not do what it says is like someone who looks at his face in a mirror and, after looking at himself, goes away and immediately forgets what he looks like. But whoever looks intently into the perfect law that gives freedom, and continues in it—not forgetting what they have heard, but doing it—they will be blessed in what they do.

Debrief after Serving

One of my professors in graduate school often remarked to his students, "Contrary to popular opinion, experience is not the best

133

teacher. Evaluated experience is the best teacher. You can have the same experience for thirty years and make the same errors. Without evaluation, all you get is the same problems and the same results."

Performance without evaluation leads to stagnation. You'll never make spiritual progress without getting regular feedback about your performance—as a parent, spouse, teacher, leader, laborer, or simply a person in relationship. Feedback promotes fruitfulness.

Five times in Proverbs 15 we read basically the same idea: the person who ignores correction is a fool and will never be productive, wise, or successful in life (vv. 5, 10, 12, 31–32). Verse 31 is exemplary: "Whoever heeds life-giving correction will be at home among the wise." To these proverbs we can add Zephaniah 3:1–2, where God describes Jerusalem and her oppressive leadership hundreds of years before Christ. Notice the connection between receiving correction and drawing near to God.

> Woe to the city of oppressors,
>> rebellious and defiled!
> She obeys no one,
>> she accepts no correction.
> She does not trust in the LORD,
>> she does not draw near to her God.

Most debriefing sessions tend to focus on positive experiences—what we saw God do and how we enjoyed serving. We absolutely must celebrate these things, but we must also be willing to examine ways to make improvements and correct shortcomings. This is particularly true for ongoing groups and when outcomes are specific and have the potential for doing good or harm.

I have observed a number of ministry teams and listened to the debriefing sessions. The transformation that takes place in people's lives—both in the group served and in the group serving—is nothing short of remarkable. Neighborhoods are transformed. People are encouraged, and the poor begin to move out of poverty. The sick and weak are prayed for and healed, buildings are built, people find faith, children are rescued, and churches thrive. Team members grow spiritually, emotionally, and intellectually. They are never the same.

The Ministry of the Towel: Don'ts

Let's move from the dos to some important don'ts.

Don't Grab Someone Else's Towel

It's tempting to do someone else's ministry because we admire their gifts or the impact they have or because we think we can do it better. I remember when a supervisor challenged me, "Bill, why do you spend most of your time doing things you're not very good at? And why do you spend so little time performing the kinds of ministry tasks you're gifted for? Why do you waste so much energy trying to be someone you're not?" I was trying to use someone else's towel.

There's a subtle message in 2 Timothy 4:5 as Paul mentors his protégé. See if you can spot it: "But you, keep your head in all situations, endure hardship, do the work of an evangelist, discharge all the duties of your ministry." Paul does not tell Timothy to discharge the duties of someone else's ministry. He says *your* ministry. Each of us has been given duties related to *our* ministry. What are your duties? What has God uniquely gifted you for and called you to accomplish? Are you constantly trying to prove yourself because you want a bigger towel, a more significant role, or a larger box on the organizational chart? When you view your gifts as less popular or desirable compared with those of others, you will tend to envy people and despise your valuable talents and skills.

Envy is the enemy of ministry because we are always looking at the wrong person, seeking the wrong opportunity. The needy people around the corner are overlooked while we stare at the award-winning homes on the street. We fail to see the woman with the flat tire because we are drooling at the Rolls Royce in our rearview mirror.

It's not much different with ministry opportunities. A graduate student looks for an internship in the city because "everyone is doing urban ministry." That's where the missional action is. She waits five months, but nothing materializes. Meanwhile, her home church needs help and might be open to the idea of her working there part-time. But she never asks—it does not even cross her mind. Her eyes are fixed elsewhere. She doesn't see the towel Jesus is holding out to her because she's looking right past it to the one she wants to use.

Don't Wait Until Your "Gift" Is Needed

"I'd really like to help get the house ready for the meeting, but I don't have hospitality gifts."

"Me, lead a small group? I don't have the gift of shepherding."

"I just don't know how you do all those hospital visits. I would be terrible at that kind of ministry. After all, I have leadership gifts, not mercy gifts."

You've probably heard these types of excuses many times. Maybe you've made similar comments. I know I have. Though I might not say it publicly, too often I think, *That's not my area of ministry*. Even when there is plenty of work to do and few hands to help, I am tempted to exhibit this selfish attitude.

The emphasis in recent decades on understanding and using spiritual gifts has been a needed correction for the church. Too many times we filled empty ministry slots with people who simply have a pulse. Thankfully, in most churches, those days are gone, but the proverbial pendulum has swung too far in the other direction. You and I don't have to have the gift of helps in order to help when help is needed. Just grab the heavy end of the log and help get it off the ground. Or, using the towel imagery, "There's mud everywhere. Grab a towel and help clean it up. Any towel will do."

In 2 Corinthians 8:1–7, we find a beautiful expression of how the church should work when needs exist. As you read this, recall that Paul has already sent a letter to the Corinthian church exhorting them not to be ignorant about spiritual gifts. Here he challenges them to give generously, citing the example of another church.

And now, brothers and sisters, we want you to know about the grace that God has given the Macedonian churches. In the midst of a very severe trial, their overflowing joy and their extreme poverty welled up in rich generosity. For I testify that they gave as much as they were able, and even beyond their ability. Entirely on their own, they urgently pleaded with us for the privilege of sharing in this service to the Lord's people. And they exceeded our expectations: They gave themselves first of all to the Lord, and then by the will of God also to us. So we urged Titus, just as he had earlier made a beginning, to bring also to completion this act of grace on your part. But since you excel in everything—in faith, in speech, in knowledge, in complete earnestness and in the love we have kindled in you—see that you also excel in this grace of giving.

Paul does not say, "Those of you who have the gift of giving, please consider making a generous contribution to the offering I am collecting for the Jerusalem church." He's asking the entire Corinthian church to participate in this opportunity to give and calls it a "service" in the body of Christ.

Let's check our hearts. What is standing in the way of us giving ourselves to others or to an uncomfortable task simply because it's not in our wheelhouse? Ego? Pride? Reputation? Fear of failure? Fear of success (I might be asked to help again)? A lack of compassion?

How willing are we to share our hearts and minds and hands in the service of others?

Don't Shove Your Towel in Someone's Face

Sometimes service is more important to those serving than to the people being served. Not everyone wants help when we want to give it, or they don't want the kind of help we are offering for the situation they are facing. We cannot pretend to know what people truly need. We must be discerning and respectful.

My father passed away in 2007. He was a kind and generous man who was six foot two and 250 pounds and had a tender heart for the poor, the weak, and the needy. But when he wanted to do something, just try stopping him. At times he was impulsive, though this tendency was usually entertaining. One evening at dinner I was eating my steak, and Dad insisted on putting salt on it. I kindly told him that it tasted just fine. "No, it'll taste much better with some salt on it," he insisted.

Once again I reiterated, "No thanks, Dad. I really like it without the salt."

Despite hearing what I had just said, Dad immediately responded, "Here, let me put some salt on it for you." I had to cover the steak with both hands, look him in the eye, and threaten to slap him with a restraining order, forbidding him to see his grandchildren for the rest of his life. I knew that would do the trick.

I was wrong.

"Are you sure you don't want some salt? Taste a piece of my steak. I'm not kidding. It really is much better." And he proceeded to put a slice of his steak on my plate.

Finally, I relented. (Now I visit my cardiologist every six months as a precaution.)

While this story is humorous, shoving a towel in someone's face is not. Even when the needs are obvious and the solutions seem crystal clear to us, it is almost never appropriate to serve others against their will. You will lose their respect and perhaps the opportunity to serve on a more extended basis in the future.

Once I watched an overzealous servant attempt to lay hands on a woman in order to pray for her. It was clear to everyone watching that she was a "hands-off" kind of person. But Prayer

Woman really wanted to put her hands on the shoulders of this businesswoman. "That's OK," she responded as she stepped back a foot or two. "We can just pray together." But you could see in the eyes of Prayer Woman that the "hands-on" strategy really mattered.

"I know you feel awkward," she said to the hands-off businesswoman. "This is probably a new thing for you. If you just let me pray for you, I promise you will never be the same."

I could sense the businesswoman thinking, *You touch me and I guarantee* you *will never feel the same!*

There they stood, powerfully communicating with very clear body language. Hands on. Hands off. A real battle of wills.

Reluctantly, the businesswoman walked away and found another team member. Sadly, Prayer Woman was clueless, assuming the woman was just not spiritually minded. It was awful. As much as we want to serve, we must respect others and use our towels wisely.

Don't Lose the Big Picture

Our service is part of a larger mission, a grander story. I find it motivating to know that what I am doing may further the cause of the gospel for many years to come. When we pray for a sick member of our small group or serve food to destitute people suffering in the barrio in São Paulo, we become a link in a long, enduring chain.

I try to remind people of this when I coach them about leading a small group in their church. The simple act of inviting someone to join the group may change lives for generations to come. You invite a single woman to a Bible study. She finds encouragement despite a dreary dating life that's void of quality suitors. Her spirits are lifted, and her attitude improves. As she becomes more whole and more confident in her faith, she feels less depressed and takes more initiative to build relationships. She finds a few new friends who introduce her to some quality guys. In six months, she has a boyfriend who loves Christ, and their relationship is growing.

I've seen it happen again and again. You never know how a little service will go a long way. A prayer, the gift of time, a warm meal, even a smile at the right time may change a heart and then a life. God has asked us to join in his redemptive work to bring good news to people. The work may be spectacular at times, but mostly it takes place during thousands of cups of coffee and hundreds of acts of kindness. Rather than allowing this to discourage us, we might see it as removing the pressure. We don't need to do all the heavy lifting; we just need to grab a towel and get it dirty.

Don't Neglect Yourself in Order to Serve Others

I realize this "don't" sounds self-oriented. That's because it is. Christians often confuse self-sacrifice and self-denial with self-destruction. Yes, Paul said, "I am being poured out like a drink offering" (Phil. 2:17; 2 Tim. 4:6). He put everything on the line for the gospel, and eventually it cost him his life. But allow me to remind you of a not-so-profound truth: you are not Paul, or Peter, or Deborah, or Mary. You are who you are.

You could never go résumé to résumé with Paul. Just look at the average American's profile when compared with Paul's.

Saul/Paul of Tarsus	Larry of Brooklyn
Jewish, single man	Married, middle-aged man
Superior rabbinic training	Failed sensitivity training
Speaks Aramaic and Hebrew, writes Greek, uses Latin for legal work	Speaks when wife lets him, fluent in locker room language, writes nothing
Persecuted the church	Goes to church on Christmas and Easter
Put people in prison	Probably should be in prison
Knocked from his horse by a bright light	Crashed his car into a traffic light
Was called to preach good news to the nations	Took a trip with his eighth-grade class to the United Nations
Was stoned for his beliefs	Was stoned, but that's another story
Was willing to die for his faith	Might be willing to diet for his faith

Sometimes we need to exaggerate the truth to see it more clearly. Hopefully, you had a few laughs at Larry's expense. Paul was given a very distinct mission for which he received very exceptional training. He lived in a different era and culture and operated under a different set of rules and circumstances. You must take the clear imperatives found in the Bible for all people and follow them faithfully. Of course, this requires sacrifice and hard work, and too few of us remember that. But the same Paul also wrote, "Pay close attention to yourself" (1 Tim. 4:16 NASB) and often had extended periods of rest and recovery after intensive seasons of ministry (while walking between towns or traveling by boat to other nations). He also didn't have social media to contend with.

Ministry is not easy, but it does not have to be destructive. Take care of yourself; we need you. God wants to use you for a lifetime. Get some rest, eat well, exercise, set some boundaries, learn when to say no, have some fun, and don't take yourself too seriously. Just take your ministry seriously when it is time to work.

So how dirty is your towel? I hope it gets its share of wear and tear and is covered with stains from effective service. When you serve in community, there should be a big pile of dirty towels on the floor, though this can pose a temptation. Some people want their towel at the top of all the other towels because they "worked the hardest" or "have been using the towel longer" or "paid more money" for their towel. Soon a hierarchy begins to emerge in the towel kingdom, and everyone wants to be king. In the next chapter, we will confront this ever-present reality.

There's only one towel at the top, and we already know whose initials are on it.

Arranging Our Towels in a Circle

I tend to stay in the shadows rather than soak up the spotlight, which means most people nudge me to the margins of their relational lives. I don't remember when I got the nickname "the younger" or, as some call me, "the less," but I certainly understand why. I cannot blame them. I don't exactly fill a room with my presence, spiritually or physically. Plus, it is hard for people in town to keep all the names straight. They confuse me with the half brother of Jesus and John's brother. Not that we look alike.

We tend to cluster in groups of four. The two sets of brothers—Peter and Andrew, James and John (sons of Zebedee)—are in the first group; Matthew, Thomas, Philip, and Nathaniel are in the second group; and the last group includes Simon the Zealot, Judas Iscariot, Thaddeus, and me. What a foursome we turned out to be. Simon and Judas have anger issues and are usually plotting something, while Thaddeus and I stay well off the radar. He's a tender fellow, a nice contrast to the big three, who could spend a little more time alone in prayer, if you ask me.

As I look around the room, I realize how grateful I am for my family. My parents, Alphaeus and Mary, never pushed me to be anything but myself. I admire their deep faith. My brother, Joses, sure loves Jesus and has been a mentor and friend, someone I can count on. I don't see why Jesus passed him up. We could sure use his maturity at the table. But no one here talks much about family, not even Jesus, even though my family and his were close at one point. Then everything got so busy—the travel, confrontations with Pharisees and Sadducees, and the crowds (oh, how I hate crowds).

So where do we go from here? Jesus knows he has my devotion, but I have little else to offer. And no one else, except Thaddeus, seems to notice I exist. James the greater, sitting on the couch near his brother, John, gets plenty of press. If you ask me, they can have it. I have no desire to be a lightning rod for every critic out there who wants Jesus's head on a platter, like that of his cousin John the Baptizer. No thanks. I don't need to be first in line or have a seat next to Jesus to feel significant. I can be small.

Small is good. Less is more. I have firsthand experience with that.

I am James "the less," son of Alphaeus.

There's a Circle at the Top

It is virtually impossible to build true community when there is rigid hierarchy or members are competing for recognition. Consider the typical management structure of a corporation, the ownership dynamics of a professional sports team, the "command and control" approach in the military, and the pastoral leadership in too many churches; you get the picture. Where you find bosses and paychecks, delegators and implementers, performance reviews and reviewers, you usually don't find much community. Enlisted troops and officers don't typically hang out any more than mail room workers and CEOs cozy up for a beer after work.

Friendships? Maybe.

Teamwork? Hopefully.

Community? Unlikely.

As you strive to build a serving community in which everyone is willing to get their towel dirty, you may encounter a quiet battle taking place. I don't mean the one you're fighting outside your community against injustice, poverty, and oppression. I mean the one inside, where you encounter pride, self-promotion, and spiritual inflation.

It is hard to build a tower out of a pile of towels, but that doesn't stop people from trying. Power-driven people will insist their towel belongs at the top. You'll recall that tower building began in Genesis 11, but *towel* building is a similar temptation. There will be bragging rights (mine is dirtier, mine is older, mine is heavier) and internal power plays (mine belongs at the front of the line, mine generates more revenue, mine has more leadership octane).

Before we let our idealism seize the day, let's be clear. In our world, governments require presidents, corporations need CEOs, and schools need administrators. But churches—and here's the big difference—have a circle of leaders. (Hang in there with me, you strong leaders. We need you. We're not done yet.)

"Appoint elders," Paul told Titus (Titus 1:5), meaning a plurality of leaders, not one überelder. The Bible teaches a shared leadership model for the church. No flying solo. No king-of-the-hill approaches to leadership. Why? Because the church is not simply a corporation with a cross on the roof.

In the church, there is a circle at the top. We were created by a circle, the Trinity. We do life together in little circles we call groups and ministry teams, and we are called to lead in a circle. Elders, deacons, leadership teams—we lead in community.

There's a circle at the top—of everything.

This does not mean that we don't need leaders or that there are no roles for strong leaders. It does mean, however, that leaders are gifted and called to serve by equipping others, delegating authority, sharing ministry, and giving away power and control to competent, emerging leaders. A one-person-controls-everything leadership model in the church is dangerous to the community and deadly to a leader.[1]

Let's Talk about Our Circle

When we serve with a circle-building mind-set rather than taking a tower-building approach, it is easier for each of us to pick up a towel without worrying about rank, power, or prestige. Here is how we ensure our circle functions well.

Mutual Submission

Ephesians 5:21 teaches us to "submit to one another out of reverence for Christ." It is actually quite an interesting statement. You would expect "submit to one another out of respect

148

for one another" or something similar. But the verse's focus is heavenward, with reverence for Christ. In other words, it is an act of worship to submit to one another. Much attention is often given to the verses that follow about the roles and relationships of men and women in the church and in the home. Godly people disagree on this issue, and it is not the intention of this book to enter the debate. My primary concern is a broader one, the practice of mutual submission to one another, as commanded here.

When we choose to submit to one another, we make a bold declaration to the world. We shout, "Enough! We are tired of fighting about who gets to wield the most power, who's bigger, better, stronger, faster!" Galatians 5:13–15 reminds us of our distinct relationship with one another as Christians.

> You, my brothers and sisters, were called to be free. But do not use your freedom to indulge the flesh; rather, serve one another humbly in love. For the entire law is fulfilled in keeping this one command: "Love your neighbor as yourself." If you bite and devour each other, watch out or you will be destroyed by each other.

A culture of mutual submission allows us to serve one another humbly in love. This does not mean no one has authority in our community. But it does mean we ask questions: How is the authority used? Who has the authority, and how much of it is shared? When all of the authority in a group rests in one person, the danger involves that person exercising power and control over the rest of the group. Instead, when authority is understood as the privilege to use power to serve the entire community, a different culture emerges; a servant culture comes to the forefront. Jean Vanier elaborates: "There are different ways of exercising authority and command: the military model, the industrial model and the community model. The general's goal is victory; the factory manager's goal is profit. The goal of the leader of a community is the growth of the individuals in love and truth."[2]

When a leader uses power and authority to manipulate a community for his or her own purposes, community is corrupted. Leaders must live in the tension that results when organizational objectives and the values of community rub up against one another. Vanier continues:

> Leaders of the community have a double mission. They must keep their eyes and those of the community fixed on what is essential, on the fundamental aims of the community. They must give direction, so that the community doesn't get lost in small wrangles, which are secondary and incidental. . . . But the leaders' mission is also to create an atmosphere of mutual love, confidence, sharing, peace and joy among the community's members. Through their relationship with individuals, through the trust shown in them, they will lead each member to trust the others. Human beings grow best in a relaxed environment built on mutual confidence. When there is rivalry, jealousy, and suspicion, and where people are blocked against each other, there can be no community, no growth, and no life of witness.[3]

How do we enter into this life of mutual submission? We journey once again to the cross. There we find our purpose and rediscover our true identity. In the upper room, Jesus was completing his preparation for the cross, his entire life and ministry having been devoted to that cause. We are part of the community of the cross, which, according to John Stott, leads to self-understanding (who we are) and to self-giving (what we are called to express to the world).

> First [is] the call to self-denial. The invitation of Jesus is plain: "If anyone would come after me, he must deny himself and take up his cross and follow me" (Mk. 8:34). . . . The self we are to deny, disown and crucify is our fallen self, everything within us that is incompatible with Jesus Christ. . . . My true self is what I am by creation, which Christ came to redeem, and by calling. My false self is what I am by the Fall, which Christ came to destroy. . . . But we must not overlook another strand in Scripture. Alongside Jesus' explicit call to self-denial is his implicit call to self-affirmation (which is not at all the same thing as self-love).[4]

Stott notes that self-denial (rejecting the false self) and self-affirmation (claiming our new identity in Christ) are both necessary.

> Neither self-denial (a repudiation of our sins) nor self-affirmation (an appreciation of God's gifts) is a dead end of self-absorption. On the contrary, both are means to self-sacrifice. Self-understanding should lead to self-giving. The community of the cross is essentially a community of self-giving love, expressed in the worship of God . . . and in the service of others. . . . It is to this that the cross consistently and insistently calls us.[5]

Jesus embraced the cross despite its shame and terror. Luke records the turning point in Jesus's earthly ministry when he began the final leg of his journey to the cross. "As the time approached for him to be taken up to heaven, Jesus resolutely set out for Jerusalem" (Luke 9:51). In the upper room, when Jesus picked up the towel, he was acting out a minidrama, a preview of what sacrificial service looks like, a precursor to the ultimate sacrifice made at Calvary.

> It was just before the Passover Festival. Jesus knew that the hour had come for him to leave this world and go to the Father. Having loved his own who were in the world, he loved them to the end. The evening meal was in progress, and the devil had already prompted Judas, the son of Simon Iscariot, to betray Jesus. Jesus knew that the Father had put all things under his power, and that he had come from God and was returning to God; so he got up from the meal, took off his outer clothing, and wrapped a towel around his waist. After that, he poured water into a basin and began to wash his disciples' feet, drying them with the towel that was wrapped around him. (John 13:1–5)

I notice two things: first, the moving phrase "loved them to the end" shows the extent and intensity of his love. Second, this act of servanthood followed by his supreme act of love on the cross were both accomplished immediately *after* "the Father had put all things under his power." That is simply stunning to me! The Father placed all the power of the universe at his disposal, so "what would Jesus do"? Not what you might expect.

Think for a moment. What does the president of the United States do immediately following the inauguration? What does a business leader do immediately after being appointed the new CEO of a company? What does an associate pastor do immediately after becoming the new senior pastor? They begin to exercise their power and authority to get things done, to move their agenda down the road. But imagine what could be done if picking up a towel was of first concern.

Imagine the president washing the feet of leaders from the opposing political party. Imagine the CEO heading straight to the mail room with his towel and basin. Imagine a new pastor moving through the aisles, washing the congregation members' feet.

Invariably, the most relevant question for us is not, "What would *they* do?" or, "What would *Jesus* do?" Rather, it is "What would *I* do with unlimited power?" It unnerves me to think about it. Mutual submission would hardly be the first thought on my mind. Yet it is our calling and our privilege. Jesus makes that clear.

Mutual Encouragement

In his compelling book *The Good and Beautiful Community*, James Bryan Smith teaches that we must distinguish between a false narrative and the true narrative for the spiritual life. The false narrative says, "The community serves my needs," while the true narrative states, "The community shapes my life." The false narrative taps into our consumerist culture and narcissistic mind-set. You see people living out the false narrative when you hear, "I wonder if this small group will help me grow?" and "I hope the sermon is good today because I really need to be fed," as well as "Why are we going to the city to do a service project when there are so many needs in our own backyard?"

Smith says,

Here is the true narrative regarding the rights and responsibilities of the community: *the community exists to shape and guide my soul. The community has a right to expect certain behavior from me, and can provide the encouragement and accountability I need. . . .* If the church has that responsibility, it also has the right to encourage certain behaviors from its members. We can and must offer forgiveness and reconciliation to all who seek it, and accept all who are broken and dysfunctional. But acceptance does not mean we ask nothing of the people who join our community.[6]

Encouragement here is not simply the act of lifting people's spirits when they are sad or downtrodden. It is the kind of encouragement we give one another to press onward in the faith. Smith refers to Hebrews 10:24–25, reminding readers that "transformation into Christlikeness has been the aim and responsibility of the church from its beginning."[7]

One of the men in our neighborhood embodies mutual encouragement. He is always thinking of the needs of others, and his actions speak louder than his words, prompting us all toward greater service. "I'm going to help Andrea move into her new home on Saturday. Since the divorce, she has so much more to handle on her own. I thought I would head over there about 9:00 in the morning and give her a hand." Without being asked, many of us soon joined him in the effort. In turn, he was encouraged and affirmed, and ultimately a family in need was served.

Mutual Accountability

As responsible members of a community, we are accountable to one another. We serve one another through mutual submission, give the gift of encouragement as we "spur one another on to love and good deeds" (Heb. 10:24), and provide mutual accountability to help us accomplish our mission and live in harmony.

Accountability is often narrowly understood in Christian circles. We talk about "accountability partners" but usually mean we want someone to keep an eye on us and call us to account when we fail. "Since you prayed only twice this week, how will you make sure you have a regular prayer time next week?" More often a statement like that makes us feel guilty. The intention is good, but sometimes the process and the relationship are misguided.

The best form of accountability is when we come alongside one another to embrace our mission and fulfill our responsibility. We don't simply provide performance feedback to one another, though feedback is necessary and helpful as part of the growth process (like a bathroom scale reveals our exact weight). We also provide resources and enter into a relationship so that together we can achieve a goal (helping us to maintain our fitness plan when we are tempted to give up).

Smith describes the kind of community we really want if progress is part of the goal:

> I want a community who will take an interest in my well-being, a community who is not afraid to ask me to make a commitment to my own spiritual growth and service to others, a community who dares to offer me a reliable pattern of transformation and then backs it up by challenging me to enter into some form of accountability in order to help me meet our commitments. I want a community who will challenge me to become who I already am: one in whom Christ dwells and delights, a light to the world,

155

salt to the earth, the aroma of Christ to a dying world. I want a community who reminds me of who I am and will watch over me with love—which means offering both comfort and warning—so that I might live a life worthy of my calling.[8]

I want that kind of community as well. And perhaps so do you. It means making a commitment to a different kind of life characterized by mutual submission, encouragement, and accountability. It means fostering a culture of humility and service in which each member eagerly picks up a towel, uses it vigorously, and then surrenders it back to the community in a spirit of self-sacrifice, not self-preservation.

Let us arrange our towels in a circle so others can see that servant leaders share their leadership in community without fear or insecurity. Let us work together in the name of Jesus, colaborers in the kingdom of God. And let us help one another to persevere.

Don't Throw In the Towel

I am torn. On the one hand, I can throw my hat in with Jesus—full time, all in, no reservations. On the other hand, I can lead my own movement or join another one. I guess I already made my decision a couple of weeks ago. It will take some recruiting and some money, but I think I can make that happen. I don't see many prospects in this room. A few guys are in the "Jesus is everything" camp, and most of the others are on the fence or simply hanging around for something big to break loose. I might win a couple of them over to my cause if I am lucky. I think I can count on Simon the Zealot, and he's got a huge network we can recruit from. We simply must do something to break this Roman yoke from our necks. Negotiations are going well with the chief priests and temple guard about the price for Jesus. Thirty pieces of silver. That's almost four months' wages!

Soon this will all be over. At times I wake up in a cold sweat. I cannot believe I am doing this. Jesus never did anything to me. But the money—there is so much I could do with that money!

Jesus has power but not the kind of political clout I was hoping for. Yes, he threw a few jabs at Herod Antipas. Calling him "that fox" took some real courage, or foolishness. I guess it depends. Unfortunately for us, Jesus has no political aspirations. Does he really believe this movement will thrive without at least conquering Judea and Galilee? Part of me is drawn to him, and I know he's chosen me. When he looks at me, I just have to turn away. He must know what is going on. He seems to know everything.

I would consider another option, but time is running out. Thirty pieces of silver. The tipping point came when he let that woman pour expensive perfume on his feet like it was water. A small fortune. That could have been sold to buy weapons and bribe politicians. I shouted, "We could use that for the poor!" to keep the others off guard. They are clueless that I am skimming funds from the treasury.

I just cannot take it anymore. I've made my decision: we have to get him out of the way. He's making more enemies every day. It should not be difficult.

Looks like we are getting close to serving dinner. Jesus is holding the bread and wine as if he has something planned. He looks so heavyhearted tonight—not his usual self. Wait, he's dipping the bread in the bowl. He's looking at me. That look. That loving, sad look. He's giving it to me. That's for the honored guest. Me? For what I am about to do?

I have to go soon. I can't stay here. This is just not for me. Thirty pieces. That is hard to pass up.

I am Judas.

Should I Stay or Should I Go?

In the upper room, the disciples began to face some of the most difficult questions in their lives. Jesus mentioned leaving, again.

He mentioned remembering him, a clue to his departure. It is likely they could not understand or chose not to. Regardless, they had to wrestle with their doubts, fears, and uncertainties. And so do we. As we seek to follow Jesus in times of fear and uncertainty, difficult questions plague us.

Will I follow Jesus fully? What does Jesus think of me, and how should I respond? Am I willing to lay down my life for him? Am I willing to trust God with my future? What if I fail him? What if our entire community falls apart? Will I have to face persecution or lose my status at work because of Jesus? Every disciple who chooses to follow Jesus is confronted with a decision: to move forward by faith or to move away, allowing fear or self-preservation to take control.

When your heart gets heavy and your life gets hard and your faith is fragile, do you consider throwing in the towel? You won't be the first one to ponder the idea. That's why we need a community. On our own, the temptation to walk away from difficult decisions and challenging circumstances—or even our faith in Christ—is just too great. During this inner struggle, we wonder if the blessing of God has been removed from us, whether we are still worthy to walk with him. Spiritual writer Henri Nouwen helps us walk this difficult path, addressing the issue with grace and truth:

The sense of being cursed often comes more easily than the sense of being blessed, and we can find enough arguments to feed it. We can say: "Look at what is happening in the world: Look at the starving people, the refugees, the prisoners, the sick and the dying. . . . Look at all the poverty, injustice and war. . . . Look at the torture, the killings, the destruction of nature and culture. . . . Look at our daily struggles with our relationships, with our work, with our health. . . ." Where, where is the blessing? The feeling of being accursed comes easily. We easily hear an inner voice calling us evil, bad, rotten, worthless, useless, doomed to sickness and death. Isn't it easier for us to believe that we are cursed than that we are blessed?[1]

It is so easy to see the trauma around us and forget our relationship with God. Can we trust the Holy Spirit one more time? Can we cling to Christ just a bit longer? Is it worth the effort to keep serving even when we see no results?

The Bible speaks to these questions with power and hope:

Do not be deceived: God cannot be mocked. A man reaps what he sows. Whoever sows to please their flesh, from the flesh will reap destruction; whoever sows to please the Spirit, from the Spirit will reap eternal life. Let us not become weary in doing good, for at the proper time we will reap a harvest if we do not give up. Therefore, as we have opportunity, let us do good to all people, especially to those who belong to the family of believers. (Gal. 6:7–10)

Let the words "we will reap a harvest if we do not give up" work themselves into your weary soul.

How many times will I invest in a difficult relationship before giving up?

How often will I serve the poor with little or no visible results?

How long will I work with a child struggling to understand the math homework before thinking this is a waste of time?

How many years will I stay at this job before I get a promotion?

These are hard questions that require discernment. We may not be able to answer how long, how often, or how many. But we can answer this question: What will happen if I give up? The answer is: nothing.

I understand what you may be thinking. *I am on the verge of burnout, weary from serving others, and even struggling with my life of faith. I have seen so much pain and agony in the world and have experienced my share of disillusionment. The last thing I need is more activity. I am already weary from doing good.* Been there, felt that.

There are two things I want to address: first, the blessings that come from perseverance and the determination to see things through to the end (as Christ did, despite great agony and emotional torment, both in Gethsemane and at Calvary); and second, the absolute necessity of creating space for renewal and replenishment both individually and as a community. Weariness of soul, disappointment with God and others, and disillusionment over unmet needs and unfulfilled expectations will wreak havoc around the table. You will resent having to pick up a towel.

The Power of Perseverance

A friend of mine owns a small business in my neighborhood. Until 2008, it was a thriving operation that provided a quality service to the community and reliable income for his family of four. I first met him in the middle of the economic downturn, and he was losing money and hope. "I am a seeker," he said with cautious laughter that revealed his spiritual uncertainty but also a spirit of adventure. "I am stuck, and I don't know how to move past this place." I offered to meet with him for breakfast to talk about his life and his business. He described his spiritual journey, his work, his family, and his relationship with his parents.

One morning early in our relationship, I asked how long he had been on this journey of faith. "Sixteen years," he said. I was impressed that he had stuck with it. He attended our church fairly frequently and had been in a small group for seekers with one of our pastors. And—here's a shocker—he tithed! I recall him saying with the logic of a businessman, "I go to the church and get something from it for me, my wife, my kids. It just makes sense to give something back for what they are giving me, so I give the 10 percent." It was so natural for him, a no-brainer. I thought about putting him on the platform the next Sunday right before we collected the offering!

He was trying to "do the right things," but he had hit a barrier. His Jewish heritage and his confusion about who Jesus really is presented stumbling blocks. Over the past sixteen years, he had met with people, attended services, and done some Bible reading. He was one of the most persistent and honest seekers I have ever encountered. By God's grace, after a year of almost weekly breakfasts and other conversations, he trusted Christ and was baptized. It was such a privilege to stand alongside him in the lake. I was grateful I had played a small role in a big drama that had unfolded over almost two decades.

Two things deeply impressed me about his story. First, his unwavering persistence was remarkable. He simply did not give up. He kept asking questions and sharing his frustrations. There were times he would say, "Billy, I just don't understand." He is over ten years younger, but I had to smile when he called me "Billy," a name only my parents and close friends from college ever used. "Why is God letting my business fail? I might lose it all. I pray to him. I ask him for help. Nothing changes." He was disheartened, and tears often accompanied his comments. "If I believe in God, will he help me with my business?"

He did not realize at the time that his failing business actually drove him to a more serious pursuit of the God who was already pursuing him. He was helpless and hopeless; God was being gentle and truthful. Which brings me to the second thing that impressed me: God's perseverance. This guy never threw in the towel, even when God appeared unreasonable and unreachable. And God never gave up on him, even when he wondered if God even cared. The greatest servant of all, Jesus Christ, is not in the business of giving up on people. He patiently, gently, and lovingly brought people and experiences into this guy's life for the entire seventeen years leading up to his baptism. Second Peter 3:8–9 is a reminder of the persistence and patience of God as he works in the hearts of people:

> But do not forget this one thing, dear friends: With the Lord a day is like a thousand years, and a thousand years are like a day. The Lord is not slow in keeping his promise, as some understand slowness. Instead he is patient with you, not wanting anyone to perish, but everyone to come to repentance.

Our God perseveres in love despite our many shortcomings and consistent wandering from him. One of my favorite congregational songs is "One Thing Remains" by Kristian Stanfill. The song describes the strength and perseverance of God's relentless love that just keeps coming our way. I love knowing that truth, and I love being reminded how nothing I ever say or do can separate me from his love.

Persistent, persevering, unfailing love is the central mark of God's character and should be of our community. That love is also the motivation for our service to others. We love because we have been loved. We serve because we have been served.

So "let us not become weary in doing good, for at the proper time we will reap a harvest if we do not give up" (Gal. 6:9).

Renewal and Replenishment

To persevere and persist never implies we neglect the rest, refreshment, and restoration required for our souls. It might be a time to step away for a season, to leave our towel hanging on the hook for a few days or even longer. There are sacred rhythms to life that must be cultivated and honored if we are to serve ourselves, our community, and our world for the long haul.

Everyone needs rest and renewal. Those in leadership roles at home, at work, or in the church must especially pay attention to the condition of their souls. Lance Witt, a seasoned pastor and leader, writes with leaders in mind when he warns:

> We all have a front-stage life and a back-stage life. Front stage is the public world of ministry. It's where we're noticed, where the spotlight is on us, where people applaud and affirm us. On the front stage everything is orderly and neatly in its place. It's where we cast vision, inspire others, and lead with skill.
>
> Front stage is all about *doing*.
>
> But we also have a back-stage life, and the two are connected.

If we neglect the back stage, eventually the front stage will fall apart. While the front stage is the public world of leadership, the back stage is the private world of the leader. The back stage is private, always dark, and usually messy. The audience isn't allowed there. Back stage has no spotlight and no glory. What happens back stage facilitates and empowers what takes place on the front stage. Back stage is all about "being."[2]

It's often been noted that we are not human *doings*; we are human *beings*. *Being* is our identity. We are men and women made in the image of God, redeemed and set apart to enjoy community with him and with one another as we serve the world. When we are confused about what we should "do" because we are not clear about who we were made to "be," we need to reclaim our identity. When it becomes impossible to "be" because our "do" is overwhelming, we need to replenish our souls.

Our community of trusted relationships is the place to bring our weariness and cries for help. It is the place to reclaim our identity and find rest. Our community will allow us to put down our towel without throwing it away forever. Here are some gifts our community can give us and we can give to others when they are on the verge of quitting.

Freedom

"It is for freedom that Christ has set us free," says the letter to the Galatian church. "Stand firm, then, and do not let yourselves be burdened again by a yoke of slavery" (Gal. 5:1). The Galatians had been freed by the gospel, but they were succumbing to the teachings of legalists who sought to weigh them down with rules and rituals that robbed them of the grace they had received in Christ. When someone in a community is tired and needs a rest from the activity of serving others, it is easy for them to listen to the wrong voices. Voices in their head condemn them, shouting, "You are lazy! You are ungrateful. All you care about is yourself. Who is going to pick up the towel if you refuse to?"

The gift of freedom releases the weary warrior from this kind of self-talk. Our encouraging voices and the loving voice of God affirm that they have served well and that it is OK to take a break. We release them from responsibility, guilt, the need to remain busy, and the false impression that they have to perform to please us or to please God.

Prayer

In our community, we offer prayers for one another, calling out to heaven for grace and mercy in times of need. The prayer of silence is also important. We sit with one another in community and listen. Henri Nouwen writes, "It is not easy to enter into the silence and reach beyond the many boisterous and demanding voices of our world and to discover there the small intimate voice saying: 'You are my Beloved Child, on you my favor rests.' Still, if we dare to embrace our solitude and befriend our silence, we will come to know that voice."[3]

Nouwen is referring primarily to individual silence and solitude, but this is just as instructive for a community. We offer a gift when we sit and pray silently in the presence of the one who is wounded. Together we listen to the still, small voice of God speaking in our hearts. There are times when our words are not necessary. It is enough simply to be. In that silence, the Spirit does a powerful work.

Joy

We take ourselves and our work too seriously sometimes. Imagine all that is happening at any given moment in the spiritual realm. Imagine intense prayers reaching up to God. Picture the power struggles with evil, the bustling activity of messengers and guardian angels, and the brutal attacks of the evil one. Yet each time a wayward and wandering sinner turns around and runs home to Christ, all heaven shifts into party mode as the angels sing and rejoice (that's my loose paraphrase of Luke 15:7).

The ancients understood that celebration was a spiritual discipline, particularly because people do not tend to practice joy and celebration when they feel otherwise. We must be intentional about celebrating one another's lives, ministries, families, and contributions to the kingdom. When we celebrate, we offer the gift of joy to the one who does not feel it at the time. A break from the mundane and dreary is just what the great Physician ordered.

John Ortberg, in his book *The Me I Want to Be*, writes:

Joyful people make us come alive.

When the book of the law was read to the people in Nehemiah's day, they were overwhelmed by inadequacy and guilt. Nehemiah gave to them and us a remarkable statement: "The joy of the LORD is your strength." We know we love joy, but we often forget the power of joy. Joy gives us the strength to resist temptation. It brings the ability to persevere. Joy is the Velcro that makes relationships stick. Joy gives us energy to love. A person who brings joy to us is an oasis in a desert land. We don't just need air and food and water. We need joy.[4]

167

We do not practice joy to mask the pain or to pretend there is no heartache. Rather, we give the gift of joy to lift someone's spirits and to remember that God is at work even in the dark places. We practice joy to bring light and hope. We do it because laughter is good for the soul. Joy allows the weary one to keep life in perspective, to remember that there are good things to celebrate because we have a good God. Joy provides the gift of relief from our momentary trials. This joy is rooted in the Triune God, and so we proclaim, "The joy of the LORD is our strength" (Neh. 8:10).

Hope

Hope has a way of suddenly bringing light and fresh air to a dark and troubled soul. We can breathe hope into one another with Scripture and song, with blessing and comfort and care, in very hands-on ways. We can share a good meal, take a walk, provide a gift card, give a shoulder massage, listen to stories, write a note, or bring little children into the room; the possibilities are endless.

For a season in life, I listened weekly to a woman share about her broken marriage and ongoing struggles with her husband's drinking. She is rooted in Christ and trusts he is at work but also knows there are things she cannot control. Each week she made steps of faith and trust, putting everything in God's hands.

Then one week her bravery was put to a formidable test. "Did anyone hear the news two days ago," she began, "about the home that exploded because of a gas leak?" It was big news, and we all nodded yes. "It was the house across the street from me in our cul-de-sac." We sat stunned as she continued. "It leveled the place, and thankfully no one was inside." She spoke calmly, saying there was much more to this story. "The force of the blast came directly across the street and struck our home. It raised our roof, shattered our windows, caved in two walls, and demolished our kitchen. I am homeless."

While tears trickled down her cheeks, she managed a tender smile. "I have seen God so clearly at work in this disaster that, crazy as it may seem, I have no worries that he will take care of us." She proceeded to describe how her daughter was miraculously protected from serious injury and how the neighbor whose home was demolished escaped uninjured, despite standing just feet away when the entire structure exploded, leaving a large crater behind. Almost immediately, a neighborhood friend offered her their home since it was up for sale and there were no buyers. "My kids can attend the same schools and be close to their friends while our home is rebuilt," she said, adding, "God is so good." Later, group members enveloped her in hugs and added to the many offers of support and help from her church and small group. A community of hope surrounded her, another gift from the God who had already been so merciful in her hour of great need.

In community, we declare that God is the source of our hope, and we share this truth with one another in tangible ways. We affirm Romans 15:13: "May the God of hope fill you with all joy and peace as you trust in him, so that you may overflow with hope by the power of the Holy Spirit."

Truth

We need to be saved from ourselves. Self-condemnation is our enemy. In community, we remind one another of the truth about ourselves. Combining the truths of John 8:44 and John 10:27–30, Brennan Manning challenges us to hear the voice of

Christ speaking those words over us, saying, "The Father of Lies twists the truth and distorts reality. He is the author of cynicism and skepticism, mistrust and despair, sick thinking and self-hatred. I am the Son of compassion. You belong to Me and no one will tear you from My hand."[5]

We claim this truth for one another when we are filled with depression and self-hatred and our weariness is overbearing. We do not ignore the pain. That too is true. But we cannot succumb to false narratives that describe us as useless failures who have nothing to offer the world. Truth is so important to a community that I devote four chapters to the subject later.

Space

Sometimes the best thing we can do for someone is to give them space. There is so much structure in our lives that we can feel hemmed in by our attempts to be present with one another, and sometimes we crowd one another. So we ask people, "Do you need someplace to be alone? Do you need to get away? Do you need some space?"

Healthy separation from work and ministry allows us to get quiet and hear the still, small voice of God. Yet even before we hear that voice, the mere sensation of stopping and resting is a gift from God. To give space also means we allow people to enter back into community when they are ready, not when we think they should be there. We might offer to check in with them, but we communicate that it is their responsibility to tell us when they want to return.

I remember speaking with a middle-aged couple at our church who had stepped aside from formal ministry for three or four months. Upon their return I asked, "What was the main reason you needed to take some time off?"

They replied calmly, "Oh, I guess we just needed some space." I had expected something like "We were burned out," or perhaps "There was a lot of conflict with people in our ministry, and we simply needed to step away." But they just wanted some space. There was no particular agenda and no overwhelming need. After many years of serving, distance was the best gift we could give them. And I did not need to ask for further explanation. That too was a gift.

Time

Similar to space is the gift of time. Space usually implies emotional distance. People must disconnect, and they usually disappear for a while. Those who need some time may also take this path. However, sometimes people simply want time not to have to do anything. They need to relinquish responsibility, let go of leadership roles, delegate tasks to others, and change their rhythms of life. They might continue meeting with their community, but they want to show up in a different way. They need time for new experiences and new reflection and to try out new gifts in the community.

The gift of time is especially needed by introverts or those who need to process things for a season. Some of us talk through our decisions. Others ponder them for days or weeks before speaking about them. Giving a weary person some time, without adding pressure to "figure it out," is a beautiful gift.

As we end this chapter, let's come back to the big idea: don't throw in the towel, no matter how hard it gets.

Kingdom work in all its forms is great, meaningful work—but very hard work. It doesn't take much for us to buckle under the demands of life and ministry in a twenty-first-century world. You may find yourself saying, "I'm spent, exhausted, and overwhelmed. If I have to meet another need, dress another wound, or give another ounce of energy to fix another problem, I am going to curl up and die!" You are tempted to call it quits, to take an extended break, or maybe to step away from the community altogether. I understand those emotions. In my darker moments, I imagine flying to a deserted island where I can just be alone, separate from everything. But quickly the fantasy fades, and I am left with the temptation to give up.

How about you? Do you wrestle with the same emotions and consider bailing out? Maybe you won't turn your back on the faith or on Jesus (though some are so battle weary they consider those options), but you do want to distance yourself from the obligations and responsibilities of serving others. If quitting has ever crossed your mind, I hope the resources in this chapter will provide encouragement and wisdom so you can persevere.

We can stay the course with a commitment to persevere in trial balanced with time for regular replenishment and renewal. We hold these in tension in community. There we share wisdom so we can all discern what we need and when we need it.

Where Do We Go from Here?

It is time to move to the third section of the book. We began at the table, where we discovered that we belong. There we learned some table manners, examined the various expressions of table fellowship we might experience, and were given guidance for telling our stories. Then, as our Master so perfectly and humbly demonstrated, we picked up a towel. We discovered our true identity as servants, learned to get our towels dirty in the messy affairs of life, and found that arranging them in a circle protects us from self-absorption and the desire for control. And we realized that the day will come when we are tempted to quit, to throw in the towel because the work is too hard or we are too exhausted. But we found many gifts to give one another to prevent that from happening.

We are learning to be disciples in the way of Jesus, enjoying his presence at the table and joining him in the unselfish ministry of the towel. Todd Hunter describes this kind of discipleship in *Christianity beyond Belief*, stating that we are

1. cooperative friends of Jesus
2. living in his creative goodness
3. for the sake of others
4. in the power of the Holy Spirit.[6]

I find myself drawn to that kind of discipleship and that kind of community. But there's a third component we must emphasize. It is not enough to enjoy table fellowship and practice mutual service. We are called to something greater. We are called to live in the truth, not satisfied simply to discuss it or debate it. At the table, we become a loving community; with towel in hand, we become a serving community.

Now let us live in the truth and become a learning community.

PART 3

Live in the Circle of Truth

There's more "truth" flying around today than there are Frisbees on a college campus. Everyone seems to have a corner on the market when it comes to the commodity we call "the truth." At the other extreme, some don't believe objective, undeniable truth exists at all. Regardless of one's view, truth language can be heard everywhere. Chances are you're familiar with a number of these phrases:

Truth be told . . .

There's not one ounce of truth in that.

Truth is stranger than fiction.

We've come to the moment of truth.

That's the gospel truth.

Truth will win the day.

The truth of the matter is . . .

If the truth were known . . .

The truth, the whole truth, and nothing but the truth.

What is truth?

There's no such thing as absolute truth (I am absolutely convinced).

Whose truth are we talking about? Yours or mine?

Let's get to the truth.

Yes, let's get to the truth! Truth is an indispensable link in the chain of community. Without it, we may experience some joy-filled camaraderie (at the local bar, for example, or on a sports team), but we will never live fully in it. Real community requires honesty, authenticity, trust, and confidentiality. None of these are possible without truth, one of the defining characteristics of any biblically functioning group, team, or relationship.

A community thrives when its members are committed to living and speaking the truth. When people are committed to relationships galvanized by love and shaped by biblical truth, a deep level of freedom emerges. Jesus affirmed this when he said, "You will know the truth, and the truth will set you free" (John 8:32)—free to be real, loving, vulnerable, honest, caring, and passionate followers of Jesus.

Conversely, oppressive management structures, dysfunctional family settings, verbally abusive relationships, and legalistic church cultures do little to foster joy-filled and dynamic community. Legalism, not freedom, reigns in such places. An abusive version of truth is used as a weapon to control or manipulate people or to gain personal power. The kind of truth that builds community builds people up and sets people free—from shame, guilt, and the sin that seeks to hold them captive.

Truth matters. It informs our identity, sharpens our minds, and softens our hearts. That same truth is often unwieldy and provocative and acts like a two-edged sword. We must wield it powerfully and handle it carefully.

Let's discover the role of truth in community life—how it shapes our table, and how it prepares us for life in the world.

A Hunger for Truth

Philip and I have much in common. We both have an introverted side to our personalities and a mild aversion to crowds (which is a problem when Jesus is around). So we are friends, in an independent kind of way. To be clear, I really enjoy relation-ships, but I'd rather have a few deep friendships than dozens of slap-on-the-back acquaintances—friends who really under-stand me, like the ones who know me by my family name, "son of Tolmai."

Jesus is the friend I have always wanted, though he has little time these days for any of us. He knows my heart, and not many men even care about that. I have a reflective side that hungers for deep spiritual conversations and wrestling with prophetic truth. Jesus understood my bent from the moment we met. I confess he caught me off guard when he said, "Here is a true Israelite, in whom there is nothing false." I had no idea how he knew me. I wondered, *How can anyone know the condition of my heart if they've never met me?*

And then it hit me. Philip was right! Granted, I could not believe anything good could come from the town of Nazareth, but I began to realize Jesus was the one who Moses was writing about. How could he be anything but the Messiah? I was not trying to impress Jesus or draw attention to myself, but suddenly I blurted out, "Rabbi, you are the Son of God; you are the king of Israel!" I simply could not contain myself.

When Jesus promised I would witness the heavens opening to reveal angels descending on the Son of Man, things really started to sound amazing. I remembered Jacob's dream in the Torah and wondered how all this fit together. From that day it has been a whirlwind of activity: healings, resurrections, calming storms, forgiving lepers, going face-to-face with Pharisees, and listening to teaching like I've never heard in my life. Above all is the simple thrill of being with Jesus almost every day.

I've been a little frustrated that I have not been offered more of a leadership role. But I trust Jesus; he knows my heart. He's known it all along, and he knows its condition today. I want to be faithful, reliable, trustworthy, tenderhearted toward the poor, committed to the truth, and willing to put truth into action. With Jesus at my side, I know I can do all these things. Yet now he's talking about going away, and it is unnerving.

But I will keep my word and remain by Jesus, regardless of what happens. I am confident in who he is and what he sees in me. My given name, Bartholomew, reminds me of my strong family heritage. My nickname, "gift of God," reminds me of my emerging spiritual destiny. That's one thing I can be sure of.

I am Nathanael.

Taste and See

Few passages of Scripture reveal a hunger for God's truth more passionately than Psalm 119. Listen as the writer describes a great longing and a desire to hear from God.

> My soul is weary with sorrow;
>> strengthen me according to your word. (v. 28)

> How I long for your precepts!
>> In your righteousness preserve my life. (v. 40)

> I have sought your face with all my heart;
>> be gracious to me according to your promise. (v. 58)

> Oh, how I love your law!
>> I meditate on it all day long. (v. 97)

> How sweet are your words to my taste,
>> sweeter than honey to my mouth! (v. 103)

> I open my mouth and pant,
>> longing for your commands. (v. 131)

> I call with all my heart; answer me, LORD,
>> and I will obey your decrees.
> I call out to you; save me
>> and I will keep your statutes.
> I rise before dawn and cry for help;
>> I have put my hope in your word. (vv. 145–47)

When we need hope and help, face temptation and trial, or encounter enemies and evil, we cry out to God. For wisdom, counsel, comfort, strength, and hope, we turn to the living Word

181

who has the Word of life. The writer here is desperate for God's truth but not because of a love for content or information. Note, the psalm does not say "the" word (or precepts or statutes or laws) but "your" word. If we love God, we naturally love his Word.

God's Word is sweeter than honey to the psalmist. Our souls are satisfied only when they encounter God. We encounter God in his Word, through the presence of the Holy Spirit at work in us, in the community of believers, and in his creative work throughout the world. If we are attentive, we can see God almost everywhere, which creates a desire to have a deeper relationship with him.

So what is the role of the Bible in our community? Why is this truth so important, and how do we use it faithfully to "build each other up" in the faith?

Read for Transformation, Not Just Information

Our spiritual growth is, in large part, informed by how we view the Bible and how we engage it in our community. There is always a tension between gathering information *from* the Word and experiencing transformation *by* the Word. The writer of Psalm 119 longs to be transformed by an encounter with God's truth, not simply informed by it. He does not say, "Teach me your precepts so that I can be smarter than the next guy" or "so that I can win theological debates and crush opponents with my arguments." He cries out, "Preserve me, strengthen me, teach me" so that he can obey and find help and hope for living.

The following chart can help us to distinguish between using Scripture in our community for information and for transformation.

How We Use Scripture

	Information	Transformation
Focus	Quantity: How far can we get?	Quality: How deep can we go?
Approach	Linear: reading for completion	Holistic: reading for understanding
Attitude	Analytical and critical: take it apart	Humble and open: take it to heart
Objective	To master the text	To be mastered by the text
Result	We study Jesus	We know Jesus
Method	Western, Bible as history: observe, interpret, apply	Eastern, Bible as mystery: listen, meditate, respond

This is not a comparison between good and bad but rather a description of how different groups use the Bible. On the left side, we tend to focus on what we do with the Bible and how much information we can cover and understand. On the right side, we focus on what the Bible does to us and how deeply it penetrates our soul. The left side focuses on content while the right side emphasizes process. The left side tends to emphasize the head while the right side emphasizes the heart. But this is not a battle between the two.

In a community, there will be people who spend more time on the left side and those who would rather stay on the right side. Our goal is not to force everyone into a 50 50 balance but to grow in our understanding of the different ways we can engage Scripture for intellectual and spiritual growth. We definitely need to know the truth before we can live the truth, but we don't want to confuse knowing the truth with living the truth.

When my daughter was young, she briefly attended a children's club whose main emphasis was Bible memory. The more you memorized, the more you were rewarded. When saying verses aloud in contests, accuracy was of supreme importance. But apparently obedience was not. My daughter revealed this shortcoming when awards were given. "C'mon up, Joey, and get your prize," announced the leader. Everyone clapped for Joey. He had memorized thirty verses this month, and kids around the room clapped and stared in amazement. Except for one—my girl.

"He's a jerk," she said.

Yikes! I sensed we had some sanctification issues going on, so I said, "Now, honey, that's not very nice."

"Yes, I know. But neither is he!" She described how Joey was a little terror when it came to treating other kids. Turns out memorizing the words "Be kind to one another" did little to help Joey be kind to others.

When truth is reduced to content, it may be more damaging than healing. For example, look at the result category on the chart with respect to Jesus. Now ponder these questions: Would I rather be studied or known? Would I rather be analyzed or understood? Would I rather be stared at or listened to? Would I rather be an object or a subject? Would I rather be treated as a person or a product? The information-only approach produces critics. The transformation-only approach produces mystics.

The Bible includes both sides, and so should our community. In discussions, we respect both sides and encourage each side to allow room for the other. Transformation-only people (zeal without knowledge) will find their experience of faith growing deeper (which is one of their great desires) when it is informed by truth. Information-only people will find their knowledge of the faith expanding (something they cherish) when they are transformed by experiencing truth.

I admire Nathanael because he was striving to live in the tension. He and Philip had knowledge of the truth (about the Messiah), but he also had an experience with truth (the living Word) that allowed him to proclaim, "You are the Son of God; you are the king of Israel" (John 1:49). He knew his Jewish history from studying the Torah, and he discovered an unfolding mystery by encountering Jesus ("You will see 'heaven open'" [John 1:51]).

What is your community like? Is it filled with left-sided people or right-sided people? Can you be a voice for living in the tension?

Ask and You Shall Receive

Living in the circle of truth means that we not only *speak* words of truth but also *seek* words of truth. We should be seekers, but we tend to be speakers. For example, we're at a dinner table or a small group or a team meeting, and the leader asks a question. Someone shares a sincere reply, which is followed by an awkward silence because no one else asks a follow-up question. Instead, three or four people share their own opinions.

I can fall into this trap as well. Sometimes I am reflecting and processing in my own head instead of responding to someone's story, comment, or question. In community, we don't ask questions in order to get answers. We ask questions to generate discussions so we can deepen our knowledge of one another. To ask, "How old were you when you lived in Pennsylvania?" is much different than asking, "What was it like growing up as a young person in Pennsylvania?" Such a question cannot be adequately answered with a simple response because it invites the respondent to tell some of their story, reflect on fond memories or serious struggles, and share more than a few words.

We say we want meaningful relationships and deeper connection, but we ask questions that don't invite people into conversation. Worse yet, when someone provides an answer, we fail to ask any questions at all. Members of the group think about their own responses instead of listening carefully to the one who's speaking. Caroline shares, "My father is older now and has begun to struggle physically, and I think he may need a walker someday." Megan replies, "I remember when my father was getting older and he needed a cane. He didn't like the idea, but we all knew he needed some kind of support."

The intent to identify with Caroline is good, but here's what Caroline actually heard Megan say: "Caroline, I am not really interested in what is going on with your father. I am interested in talking about what happened to my father. That's because my story is more important than your story." It would have been so much better to say, "I bet that must be hard for him" or "Is it difficult for you to watch him getting older?" An even more in-depth response would be, "Tell us more about your father and your relationship with him at this point in time. It sounds like you really care about him."

We settle for quick answers instead of generating robust discussions. That's because we ask the wrong kinds of questions. Too many of our questions are left-side questions—questions about information. We need to ask more right-side questions—questions about our experiences and questions that provoke transformation. Here are some pointers for shaping conversations that build relationships in community.

Seek understanding, not just information.

Tell us more about that.

Help me to understand the reason you did that.

What was that like?

I hear a lot of enthusiasm in your voice. What is giving you motivation?

Guide the conversation toward greater depth.

What would it look like if things were different than you just described?

What if this problem does not go away? What kind of decisions do you think you will have to face?

That sounds like a great idea. How do you turn that into reality?

Invite reflection.

What do you think that means?

How did that affect you? Did you find yourself angry or just frustrated?

Pursue clarity when there appears to be confusion.

What you said sounds like a contradiction. Can you clarify what you mean?

I am not sure I'm following your line of reasoning. Can you describe again what you mean?

These questions have the potential not only to generate lively conversations, deep introspection, and community engagement but also to foster real change. I have found that asking these kinds of questions does three things:

1. Creates a learning environment rather than a teaching environment. If our discussion is primarily driven by the question-answer paradigm, we tend to focus on content instead of process.
2. Encourages people to tell their stories. In chapter 4, we talked about the importance and value of storytelling around the table. As people begin to open up their lives, the right kinds of questions will create a dynamic and fruitful discussion. Asking great questions communicates to the person who is speaking that we really care about their story, that we are truly listening, and that we want to know more about their life.
3. Establishes a safe, relaxing, and conversational tone when we gather. When a discussion is primarily focused on fact finding instead of relationship building, people begin to get wary. Very few people enjoy feeling like they are being interrogated by their parents: "Did you put the trash out? What time is the dance recital? Is your homework done?" Questions that are thoughtful will create an environment for communication that fosters community.

Don't Shoot the Messenger

Sometimes, just when we think we're getting somewhere, somebody kills the discussion. Perhaps they are naive or just insensitive or have a low EIQ—Emotional Intelligence Quotient. They say something to shut down the communication. Henry Cloud and I have used the following five "discussion killers" to train leaders and help groups communicate.

Judging

A couple in your circle of truth describes a challenging interaction with their middle-school daughter. "Sarah can be pushy sometimes, but we know she's just frustrated about some difficult things at school right now, so we don't confront her about it."

"Really," says a group member. "That's not smart. It's the wrong approach. If you don't bring some discipline to that situation, you are going to have authority issues when she gets older." Instead of questions being asked, a judgment has been rendered. No attempt has been made to understand the situation or to express empathy with these parents. As a result, the conversation comes to a quick and very bad end.

Preaching

A preaching response to the same situation can sound like this: "I remember those years with our kids. It's the most awkward time! I did a lot of reading and went to a few seminars, and that helped a lot. Here's what I discovered. First, the best thing to do is to wait at least twenty-four hours before confronting her. Second, and every author I read said this, you really must make sure she knows who's in charge. You are the parent, not her." On and on the sermon goes, peppered with dozens of "you'd better" and "don't ever" statements. Just when things were starting to flow, another discussion bites the dust.

Summarizing

For some reason, certain people need closure long before a discussion comes to an end. After a barrage of advice giving and problem fixing (potential discussion killers themselves), someone jumps in and pulls it all together for everyone. "So it sounds like the next time it happens you'll deal with it right away like Mike suggested. Then you'll see how she responds, and if things go badly, you won't let her attend the next dance, which was your idea, right Karen? Seems like you have some good input from us, so now you can handle anything Sarah throws your way." Summarizers tend to think they are doing their community a great service. Instead of waiting for us to process what is happening (and "waste" the group's precious time), they wrap things up so the discussion can move on. Discussion? What discussion?

Minimizing

This one's easy to do. Just treat the situation as though it is no big deal. "Welcome to the world of parenting a middle schooler! Don't worry folks. This too shall pass. I remember how nervous we were during that stage of life. But look at our kids today. Everything's turned out just fine. Don't sweat the small stuff, because it's all small stuff!"

Spiritualizing

This is probably my biggest pet peeve in groups. People use Scripture passages or spiritual clichés to avoid real engagement with real problems and real people. "I know this situation with Sarah has you guys upset. But just remember that you're under the blood and that all things work together for good to those who are called according to his purpose. God will work out everything in its season. We'll just lay this before the Lord, claim victory in the name of Jesus, and watch him open a door in the angelic realms so that your barns fill to overflowing. Amen!" You get the idea.

Sometimes in our gatherings we have to act like traffic cops (a Henry Cloud metaphor), directing the discussion according to some healthy ground rules (recall the table manners from chapter 2). If people start using these common discussion killers, someone needs to speak up and redirect the conversation back to the speaker. "Before we all jump in with ideas and advice, please tell us more about Sarah and how we can support you both during this season." Over time, good questions will drive away bad habits, and the group will find a hunger for truth—truth about God, his Word, and one another.

Move with the Spirit

A community that hungers for truth hungers for the Holy Spirit. He is "the Spirit of truth" (John 16:13) and will guide our community into all truth. Let's remember that we are building a *spiritual* community, a place led and guided by the Holy Spirit. Truth is so important to God that he gave us a book, the Bible, and he gave us a person, the Spirit. In the upper room, Jesus wanted his followers to have clarity about the ministry of the Holy Spirit among them as a group.

If you love me, keep my commands. And I will ask the Father, and he will give you another advocate to help you and be with you forever—the Spirit of truth. The world cannot accept him, because it neither sees him nor knows him. But you know him, for he lives with you and will be in you. (John 14:15–17)

But the Advocate, the Holy Spirit, whom the Father will send in my name, will teach you all things and will remind you of everything I have said to you. (John 14:26)

When the Advocate comes, whom I will send to you from the Father—the Spirit of truth who goes out from the Father—he will testify about me. (John 15:26)

When he comes, he will prove the world to be in the wrong about sin and righteousness and judgment: about sin, because people do not believe in me; about righteousness, because I am going to the Father, where you can see me no longer; and about judgment, because the prince of this world now stands condemned. (John 16:8–11)

But when he, the Spirit of truth, comes, he will guide you into all the truth. He will not speak on his own; he will speak only what he hears, and he will tell you what is yet to come. (John 16:13)

These passages make it clear that the primary ministry of the Holy Spirit is to glorify Christ. "His chief purpose," says biblical scholar Merrill Tenney, "is not to make himself prominent but to magnify the person of Jesus. The Spirit interprets and applies the character and teaching of Jesus to the disciples and by so doing makes him central to their thinking. He makes God a reality to people."[1] Tenney comments on John 16, observing that there are three major aspects of this Jesus-focused ministry of the Spirit:

1. The Spirit brings conviction of sin, righteousness, and judgment to the world, demonstrating our need for salvation. In a spirit of grace and truth, our community declares the good news of the gospel in word and deed, calling people whom we love to turn back to God for forgiveness, reconciliation, and freedom from judgment.

2. The Spirit supplies guidance, clarifying our direction as a community and helping us to understand and practice the truth. Jesus departed so that he and the Father could send us his Spirit, now dwelling in us individually and among us as a community. We are now empowered to make wise decisions and fulfill our ministry in the world.

3. The Spirit reveals Jesus more perfectly to and through those who represent him. When people see the community of Jesus—inviting people to the table and humbly picking up a towel—they are seeing Jesus at work.[2]

Our hunger for truth is ultimately a hunger for intimacy with the Triune God. The Spirit works in and through us, points us to Christ, and confirms we are loved by the Father. The presence of the Spirit in our community makes God real to us. We watch him change lives, heal wounds, bring people to repentance and faith, and teach us how to live out the Word. He provides direction and guidance for our community.

Telling Ourselves
the Truth

I am not as skeptical as some believe or as naive as others may think. Sometimes I can be too pessimistic, and I certainly have my share of doubts about this whole group. But who wouldn't? When I look around the room, I see some very unreliable characters. Across from me sits a zealot, a tax collector, a few gung ho "let's take over the world" types, and at least one steely-eyed crook (I picked him out the first month we were together). Jesus seems to trust them, but I just cannot. The facts speak for themselves.

Frankly, it is getting harder for me to trust Jesus. Don't get me wrong. I have faith in his character and am in awe of his power. He is a great teacher and might even be the Messiah, though as I look at the data, I am not convinced. I have heard and seen some amazing things. We all have. But lately I've been worried. Jesus has been talking about dying and suffering and leaving. Just a few moments ago he said, "Little children, where I am going you cannot come," and then to Peter, "but you will follow later." Which is it? Can we follow or not? I needed clarity, so I asked, "Lord, we don't know where you are going, so how can we know the way?" He answered that he was the way. But the way to what? Where? How? Never any details; never enough information.

I'm sure Jesus knows that deep down inside I would do anything for him. When he told us he was headed back to Bethany to "wake up" his deceased friend Lazarus, the others were filled with fear and disbelief. After all, people had tried to stone Jesus there. I didn't like the idea either. But I said, "Let's go also, so that we may die with him." Some thought I was being sarcastic. But really, I was ready to go wherever Jesus wanted to go, even if it meant we would die along with him. So despite what others think, I am committed. I don't have any problem with Jesus, but some of the guys at the table really bother me.

I hesitate because we just don't have enough information, and the situation is getting tense. Can't anyone else see this? The crowds are larger; the politicians are bolder; and the religious leaders are angrier. It's a powder keg. In the midst of it all, Jesus remains vague and elusive, saying he will all understand in due time. Why not now? Why can't he just lay all the cards on the table so we can prepare? I'd like to pass it along to my twin brother so he can tell our family back home. Whatever is coming, I want to be ready.

I love Jesus; I just want some clarity. Is that too much to ask? My confidence grows when I have the inside story and when I can see things firsthand. Then I can make a wise decision. That's when I'm ready to act. Just give me the facts.

I am Thomas.

Mirror, Mirror

In this day and age, we have more sources than ever from which to glean information. Popular options include television news, newspapers (while they're still around), e-newsletters, word of mouth, books, magazines, satellite news channels, blogs, discussion groups, and good old gossip. But how do we judge reliability? Who tells us what is really true about the world and about ourselves? Can we trust our own judgment? Thomas tried that, and it created more confusion than clarity.

I have a lovely daughter, eighteen at the time of this writing. As she heads off to college, her identity will be shaped by the books she reads, the people she listens to, and the truth she believes about how the world views her and about how God sees her. She is a woman of great strength, inspiring beauty, and formidable wit, yet I know she will encounter false messages from the culture about her true identity.

Internet poet Richard Lamoureux confronts the lies women are told about their true identity, calling them to celebrate their real selves in a poem called "The Mirror Is a Liar."[1] Lamoureux confronts the lies told by the wrong kind of mirror, a mirror that distorts a woman's beauty and tells her she is less than acceptable unless she wears the right clothing and makeup. But there is another mirror—one that reflects the beauty of her soul and her true identity within.

Lamoureux captures a great truth: women can be looking in the wrong mirror, one designed by the beauty industry to reflect what women "should" look like. He wants women to look in a different mirror, a real mirror. So do I. And I also want men to discover and claim their true selves. We too are bombarded with images and information describing who we should be. We need a true mirror, says the poet.

We need to tell ourselves the truth.

We need a true mirror in our spiritual lives as well. A place we can look that gives us true feedback about our condition and our identity. The Bible says that God desires "truth in the innermost being" (Ps. 51:6 NASB).

How do we bring truth into our innermost being? Where do we find an accurate reflection of who we are? Where do we discover reality about ourselves, about God, and about the world? Followers of Jesus have been given two mirrors that reveal our human condition and our heavenly position: Scripture and community.

Scripture

The Word of God serves as a mirror, reflecting back to us the truth we desperately seek. James says:

> Do not merely listen to the word, and so deceive yourselves. Do what it says. Anyone who listens to the word but does not do what it says is like someone who looks at his face in a mirror and, after looking at himself, goes away and immediately forgets what he looks like. But whoever looks intently into the perfect law that gives freedom, and continues in it—not forgetting what they have heard, but doing it—they will be blessed in what they do. (James 1:22–25)

The Bible speaks to the human condition and gives us an accurate picture of who we were before our salvation and who we are after. In the 1800s, Danish philosopher and theologian

Søren Kierkegaard said, "When you read God's Word, you must constantly be saying to yourself, 'It is talking to me, and about me.'"[2]

The Word is speaking to us and about us, revealing that we were lost, wayward, rebellious, self-centered, and headed for destruction. But now we are forgiven and freed from sin's rule, justified, set apart for God, equipped, empowered, indwelt by the Spirit, blessed, gifted, friends with God, called for a purpose, and assured of eternal life with Jesus and his followers.

Can you recall the first time you encountered the Bible in a way that rocked your world? I became a follower of Jesus on Christmas Eve 1981, about eighteen months after college graduation. After hearing of my newly formed faith, a high school football buddy invited me to his small group. I will always be grateful to him and his wife for their unselfish contribution to my early formation, my decision to leave banking and attend seminary, and my love for the Word of God. As I entered their home that first evening, I was greeted by a dozen young men and women at various levels of spiritual maturity and commitment to Christ. We opened the Bible to 1 Timothy and began to read, reflect, pray, and grow.

I will never forget that first group and the spiritual adrenaline rush I experienced as we studied the Word in community and it became real and alive to me for the first time in my life. There I discovered who I was, in what ways I was gifted, how I was called, and the new person in Christ I was becoming. The mirror of truth was shaping me, challenging me, cleansing me, and guiding my every step. I was so passionate about the Bible that I soon purchased an entire New Testament commentary series and spent many evenings reading Scripture and poring over the notes in the commentaries. My parents thought I'd jumped off a cliff—and they were right. I had dived headlong into the Word and was drowning in the truth.

I learned something, however, during that season of explosive personal growth, something that has become one of my guiding principles for studying the Word of God: learn to study the Bible *for* yourself, but never study it *by* yourself. Certainly, daily reading of the Bible is one of the core spiritual practices every follower of Jesus should master. But don't stop there. Reading and studying the truth in community will make the mirror of truth much clearer and brighter. Input about the text from others, including Bible interpreters throughout the ages and those sitting alongside you, will sharpen and shape you far beyond anything you can do alone.

The Bible can be trusted as a compelling mirror because it is reliable, authentic, and trustworthy—the very words of God given to us for our salvation, growth, and success in the world (Josh. 1:7–8; Ps. 1; Rom. 1:16). It was written by over forty authors on three continents over a period of fifteen hundred years and is remarkably consistent. The words were recorded by people from all walks of life, including poets, prophets, teachers, physicians, scribes, kings, farmers, fishermen, warriors, shepherds, and business leaders. Each was guided by the Holy Spirit to ensure that the words were accurate and aligned with the purposes and will of God (2 Tim. 3:16; 2 Pet. 1:20–21).

In the upper room, Jesus spent a good portion of the evening speaking the Word to his followers, just as he had done throughout his ministry. Because he is the living Word, his words are God's Word. Eight times he uses the phrase "I tell you the truth" to signal that his Word is true and of supreme importance to this community, just as it is to yours and mine.[3] While a few of Jesus's comments were directed specifically to Judas and Peter (concerning Judas's betrayal and Peter's denial), he spoke truth to the entire group. Let's look at these comments and the primary focus of each as it relates to community. I offer these insights alongside what you can glean from each of these passages as you study them with others.

"Very truly I tell you, no servant is greater than his master, nor is a messenger greater than the one who sent him" (John 13:16).

We must be clear about the relationship between servant and master. Even as he serves, Jesus is our Master. He is our Lord, Teacher, King, and Savior. Despite the power and the authority that he entrusts to his community, we must always remember who is Lord and who is not. Christ modeled full obedience to the Father while he was on earth so that we can understand the relationship between a servant and his master.

As Christ was fully obedient to his Father, we are called to practice full obedience to Christ, following his example. One of the greatest things we can do in our community is to read and reflect on the Word and then motivate one another to put it into practice.

In community, we help each other practice the Word of truth so that lives change—ours as well as those of others around us.

"Very truly I tell you, whoever accepts anyone I send accepts me; and whoever accepts me accepts the one who sent me" (John 13:20).

To "accept" Christ means to believe by faith that his sacrificial death on the cross saves us, but a broader meaning is also implied here. When we have a relationship with Jesus, we have a relationship with the Father because the Son came to reveal the Father. To accept Jesus is to accept the Father (and the Holy Spirit) because we enter a relationship with the Triune God. We do not merely accept Jesus's teaching or his redemptive work on our behalf—we receive him!

Pause to pray when you gather and acknowledge that Jesus is present and that you want to accept all he has to offer you.

"Very truly I tell you, whoever believes in me will do the works I have been doing, and they will do even greater things than these, because I am going to the Father" (John 14:12).

As followers of Christ, we will do greater works in this world than Jesus was able to accomplish. How? Because when he departed, he sent the Holy Spirit to indwell and empower believers. Jesus could not be present physically throughout the entire world, but now, by his Spirit, his presence and power are multiplied through his church. In this way, greater works are being accomplished. Though not greater in intensity (how can we exceed raising the dead and walking on water?), our works are greater in scope and frequency.

Henri Nouwen says that the greatest work we can do is to give our lives to one another and to the world. Maybe that is what makes real community so irresistible: the sight of men and women giving of themselves to one another in love.

When we think about our being given to each other, what comes immediately to mind are our unique talents: those abilities to do special things especially well. . . . However, when focusing on talents, we tend to forget that our real gift is not so much what we can do, but who we are. The real question is not "What can we offer each other?" but "Who can we be for each other?" . . . It is the gift of our own life that shines through all we do. As I grow older, I discover more and more that the greatest gift I have to offer is my own joy of living, my own inner peace, my own silence and solitude, my own sense of well-being. When I ask myself, "Who helps me most?" I must answer, "The one who is willing to share his or her life with me."[4]

"Very truly I tell you, it is for your good that I am going away. Unless I go away, the Advocate will not come to you; but if I go, I will send him to you" (John 16:7).

We have an advocate, someone to represent us and pray for us and comfort us. That person is the Holy Spirit. Every community needs to look to the Holy Spirit for guidance and for power.

Jesus replied, "Anyone who loves me will obey my teaching. My Father will love them, and we will come to them and make our home with them. Anyone who does not love me will not obey my teaching. These words you hear are not my own; they belong to the Father who sent me. All this I have spoken while still with you. But the Advocate, the Holy Spirit, whom the Father will send in my name, will teach you all things and will remind you of everything I have said to you." (John 14:23–26)

When we gather, we need to be aware that the Spirit is at work teaching, guiding, and comforting us as we meet in Jesus's name and embrace the truth. I have felt his power and presence many times in a small group or when praying with a close friend.

He whispers and reminds me of Jesus's teachings, way of life, and promises.

"Very truly I tell you, you will weep and mourn while the world rejoices. You will grieve, but your grief will turn to joy" (John 16:20).

The disciples will mourn at the death and departure of Christ. But after the resurrection, their grief will turn to joy. In contrast, the world—those who put Christ to death—will rejoice at first, but then they will grieve when they understand they put the Son of God to death.

The disciples needed hope and so do we. Loss, death, and tragedy flood our lives with grief and despair. We need to believe. We need to know that there is light at the end of the tunnel— the assurance that after trauma and trial there will be joy and relief and celebration. God promises these things for every believer. Some people will experience them here on earth, while others will enjoy this fullness only in the new heaven and the new earth.

The truth that Jesus gives us is truth for the long haul, not simply truth for the moment to help us meet life's immediate problems and concerns. Big truth prepares us for big problems and gives us confidence by showing us the big picture. I find that chapters in the Bible like Revelation 22 provide an eternal perspective and enduring hope. Here are a few verses I find encouraging:

> Then the angel showed me the river of the water of life, as clear as crystal, flowing from the throne of God and of the Lamb down the middle of the great street of the city. On each side

of the river stood the tree of life, bearing twelve crops of fruit, yielding its fruit every month. And the leaves of the tree are for the healing of the nations. No longer will there be any curse. The throne of God and of the Lamb will be in the city, and his servants will serve him. They will see his face, and his name will be on their foreheads. There will be no more night. They will not need the light of a lamp or the light of the sun, for the Lord God will give them light. And they will reign for ever and ever. (Rev. 22:1–5)

It is not unusual for dying believers to ask for Scripture to be read to them. Familiar passages include Revelation 22 as well as Psalm 23, the Beatitudes in Matthew 5, and John 14:1–3. These passages galvanize the community around truth and bring comfort and encouragement to those who need it most.

"Very truly I tell you, my Father will give you whatever you ask in my name" (John 16:23).

Jesus encourages his community to go to the Father in prayer at any time. Whatever we ask in the name of Jesus—that is, whatever is in accordance with his will and the truth of his Word—the Father will provide.

Jesus knew that he would be leaving his followers very soon. So he gave them assurance that if they cried out to the Father, he would hear them. And if they prayed according to God's will, he would supply their every need.

Our community needs to know that same assurance. Thomas relied on his own self-confidence, rooted in facts he could touch and feel and see. Who needs prayer when you have all the information before you? Prayer is for people of great faith.

The Bible is a clear, compelling mirror. It reflects truth back to us at all times. It is never foggy, never scratched from wear, and never needs to be polished. It is already pure. We simply need to look into the Word and let it show us who we really are and tell us the grand dream we are called to fulfill. It is our first mirror. The second mirror that brings us clarity and reflects fully the life Christ has called us to walk together is community.

Community

In Scripture, we discover the words of truth; in community, we practice the works of truth. Scripture tells us how to live; our community tells us how we are really living. The Word provides spiritual feeding; our community supplies spiritual feedback.

The Bible teaches us to give one another wise counsel and truthful feedback. That's how we accomplish the many "one anothers" listed in Scripture.

Brothers and sisters, if someone is caught in a sin, you who live by the Spirit should restore that person gently. But watch yourselves, or you also may be tempted. (Gal. 6:1)

Therefore each of you must put off falsehood and speak truthfully to your neighbor, for we are all members of one body. (Eph. 4:25)

Therefore encourage one another and build each other up, just as in fact you are doing. Now we ask you, brothers and sisters, to acknowledge those who work hard among you, who care for you in the Lord and who admonish you. Hold them in the highest regard in love because of their work. Live in peace with each other. And we urge you, brothers and sisters, warn those who are idle and disruptive, encourage the disheartened, help the weak, be patient with everyone. (1 Thess. 5:11–14)

In *Making Small Groups Work,* Henry Cloud and John Townsend list several benefits of giving one another mutual feedback in the context of a community. The list includes recognition of gifts, correction of faults, and the alignment of our self-image with God's reality. Community-oriented groups and teams can accomplish these things because they create an environment for loving feedback. Regarding this feedback, Cloud and Townsend note,

> Your group members should see it as their task to understand what the rest of the group sees about them regarding:
>
> • Feelings, attitudes, values, and spirituality
> • Behaviors, patterns, self-destructiveness, weaknesses, needs, and pain
> • Limitations, pride, arrogance, and sinfulness
> • Talents and abilities
> • Communication and relational styles[5]

We may find this kind of community feedback awkward and uncomfortable at first, but eventually we will see the value and learn the process of giving it to one another. If there is an environment of truthfulness and safety, of really being "for one another" instead of in competition with one another, the culture is ripe for this kind of experience.

I remember speaking in a men's group about some failures in my life and how I wanted to get beyond them. After I rambled for a few minutes, a wise member of the group (who can sometimes be a "wise guy") sarcastically replied, "Well, it's a good thing you're not a perfectionist or obsessive-compulsive." The guys laughed hysterically, but then his comments took a more serious turn. "Bill, I've heard you talk about this many times. We've been over this ground before. You have very high expectations for yourself and often view yourself as not very successful. You must step back and look at what God has done in your life over the last ten years." After describing a number of successful projects and initiatives I had completed and offering some gracious feedback about my family, he said, "You need to live more in the present and be less preoccupied with the future. God is at work in you now, and when the time is right, doors will open. So stop banging your head against them."

His words rang true and generated additional affirmation by the group. Sometimes we need a community to reflect back to us what they are seeing in our lives. Are we really putting biblical principles to work? Do we talk of good theology but not walk it? Are we willing to let others mirror how they experience us, giving feedback about our attitudes, actions, idiosyncrasies, fears, and insecurities? If not, why not?

We Mirror God to the World

What do people see when they look at our community, listen to our conversations, and observe our behaviors? Do they see judgment, disinterest, self-righteousness, arrogance, self-sufficiency, or aloofness? Or do they see in us love, joy, acceptance, truthfulness, care, interest, and a sense of welcome?

Brennan Manning quotes Keith Miller describing the early church in *The Scent of Love*:

> The early Church grew "not because of the [spiritual gifts] of Christians—such as the gift of speaking in tongues—and not because Christianity was such a palatable doctrine (to the contrary, it is about the most unpalatable doctrine there is) but because they had discovered the secret of community":
>
> ". . . There was something about the way they spoke to one another, about the way they looked at one another, about the way they cried together, the way they laughed together, the way they touched one another that was strangely appealing. It gave off the scent of love. The onlooker . . . would listen some more, still not understanding, and start to drift away again. But again he would be pulled back, thinking, I don't have the slightest idea what these people are talking about, but whatever it is, I want part of it."[6]

Sounds irresistible. But only to the lonely, broken, needy, weak, and outcast members of the ragamuffin class.

Just a few weeks ago I saw a young man wearing a T-shirt that said, "Show me, don't tell me!" The world needs a show-and-tell approach to truth. We simply cannot emphasize one over the other.

We study the truth for ourselves in Scripture, and we apply the truth to ourselves in community. When we are willing to look into these two mirrors with honesty and humility, we become a community for the world. A rising generation of young adults is listening to what we say and watching what we do. What are they hearing and seeing?

Truth is not a subject we study; truth is a people we become.

The Truth Hurts,
the Truth Heals

I watched as he healed Peter's mother-in-law. I was there when he raised Jairus's daughter from the dead. I stood on the mountain when Moses and Elijah appeared; he was transfigured before our eyes, and the voice from heaven said, "This is my Son, whom I have chosen; listen to him." From the beginning, I saw his power in everything he said and did (frankly, that is about all I could see). And I wanted that power. Growing up in the fishing business, I didn't have much influence over others. We were just ordinary people doing ordinary work. Then he came along, and that changed forever. He wielded spiritual strength and relational clout.

Despite my craving for power, he has always loved me. And he still does. Even when I blow it. I remember when we went to Samaria and they rejected our Good News. My brother and I wanted to destroy the city with fire. We had ignored his teaching about humility, even after he had put a child on his lap to teach us the true nature of the kingdom. How arrogant we were! We even thought we were worthy to drink his cup—that we could do the mission he was called to complete. How utterly pompous!

It all came to a head when my brother and I tried to negotiate the best seats at his kingly table after he finally gains control and sets up his government. Everyone was furious with us, but what did I care? I was such a fool. Then he said that he came not to be served but to serve, a clear rebuke to us all. That truth hit me right where it hurt most—my pride.

Ironically, I did get the best seat at this table, right next to Jesus. But it is not how I expected it to be. I don't feel like I'm in charge; all I feel is his love. That's what stands out most to me. I have felt more of his love these last weeks than ever. So now I've been thinking of myself as " the disciple whom Jesus loves" more than "the one who gets the best seat." Of course, he loves all of us. But it's most amazing that he loves me.

Yes, Jesus loves me—me, the power monger; me, the city destroyer; me, one of the "sons of thunder"; me, the one who wants the best seat in the house. I am the disciple Jesus loves.

I am John.

It Cuts Like a Knife, but It Feels So Right

I taught with Henry Cloud and John Townsend for a number of years as we partnered to help church leaders train their small group teams. I remember a powerful illustration Henry used to depict the way truth penetrates our souls. "A man wearing a mask walks toward you, renders you unconscious, thrusts a knife into your body, and takes your money. If this happens in a dark alley, we call him a criminal. But if this takes place in a hospital, we call him a surgeon. Either way you lose some money; but one wants to hurt you, and the other wants to heal you."

The truth can cut like a knife. It can be a weapon, much like a sword. "The sword of the Spirit, which is the word of God" is part of the armor of God in Ephesians 6 and can be used to hurt, in this case the enemy (v. 17). But the truth can be another kind of sword, one that cuts into you, not into your enemy. Hebrews 4:12 reminds us, "For the word of God is alive and active. Sharper than any double-edged sword, it penetrates even to dividing soul and spirit, joints and marrow; it judges the thoughts and attitudes of the heart." Jesus used this sword to rebuke John and James when they suggested destroying the Samaritans for not receiving their gospel message (Luke 9:51–56).

In a thriving community, the truth may hurt even as it heals. The more time we spend with one another, the more likely the words of Scripture and the words we share will be used by the Spirit to penetrate our souls, revealing the true condition of our hearts.

Let the Truth Get in the Way

Mark Twain once quipped, "Don't let the truth get in the way of a good story." He was right. It can ruin everything. It can wreak havoc on compulsive lying, expose ulterior motives in a business negotiation, and root out distortion and exaggeration in a conference talk. In a community of Christ followers, the truth can destroy our false understanding of God, and that's a very good reason to let the truth get in the way.

When we engage the truth in the context of genuine table fellowship, we help one another gain clarity concerning our views of God, self, and others. Truth be told, we embrace a number of false narratives about God, ourselves, and others, and these must be confronted with the healing (and perhaps painful) scalpel of truth.[1]

A False View of God

Our view of God may be shaped by a number of factors: how we view our earthly father, teachings from various churches, personal experiences with God, life circumstances, and expectations about what God is like. If our lives have been filled with negative life experiences and misunderstandings about God, we would expect our views concerning God's character and actions to be inaccurate. Here are some common misperceptions about God, rooted in our own misguided impressions and ideas.

An uninterested boss. We think, *God does not know me. I must perform to get his attention. He doesn't know my pain, he doesn't know my joys, he doesn't understand my story, so I must do something to get noticed.*

While in graduate school, I worked for a big church with a large Sunday school ministry. I helped launch a class that reached out to businesspeople who had questions about God. In a couple of months, the class had twenty-five regulars. One day, a church leader asked how many church members were in the class. I said there were none because the class was focused on reaching people far from God or who did not attend church. I mentioned that many were not Christians, and a few had very bad church experiences. We were hoping to lead them to Christ or reconnect them with the church. He then replied, "Right. And how many church members do you have?" I repeated my explanation, but he asked the same question. This continued for some months until one day I simply listed all twenty-five class attendees as "members" on my next class report. I had no idea the effect this would have.

The next morning I received a call telling me that the senior pastor wanted me to participate in the Sunday service. That Sunday he called me to the platform and told the congregation what a "fine job this young man is doing with our class of businesspeople. We now have twenty-five new church members!" Performance matters. Nothing had changed in the class—no new believers, no recommitments to the faith—but now I was a hero. I had signed up twenty-five new members!

Pleasing people and impressing God are hard work. But that is not what God wants. God wants us to be his friends. "Here I am! I stand at the door and knock. If anyone hears my voice and opens the door, I will come in and eat with that person, and they with me" (Rev. 3:20). Jesus is inviting us to the table, not the arena.

An unresponsive father. A persons thinks, *God doesn't hear me. He is here but not really connected or attentive.* This is like a friend who says, "My dad sits in the living room watching television and reading the paper, but he's unaware I am here in the room. I make a comment and he grunts but doesn't really respond."

We may feel this way toward God because he seems irresponsive to our prayers. He must not care, or he's too busy, preoccupied with world hunger and the conflict in the Middle

East. We judge God by the results we see, not the relationship we have. No reply means he has checked out of our life. God, however, speaks to us on his terms, not ours. He says, "Be still, and know that I am God" (Ps. 46:10). He is present and silently at work, yet we perceive him as an inattentive parent. We project our disappointing family experience onto God.

A pastor describes the final moment with his father before he left for college. As he offered a final good-bye, his dad just sat there, his face covered by the newspaper he was reading. "OK, Dad, I'm headed out now." Without lowering the paper, his father replied, "OK." That was it. No hugs, no eye contact, no apparent interest. Consequently, this pastor struggled for many years with performance issues and with an obsession for perfectionism. He worked so hard to please God that it wore him out. Trying to pry a response out of an inattentive God is extremely hard work.

An unmerciful judge. According to this view, we may think, *God's love is conditional. I don't feel loved by God. Therefore, I must have done something wrong to merit the judgment of God. I am surely his enemy. I will be punished, and I deserve it.*

People with this view are usually plagued by pain and anger. They tend to act out in unhealthy ways. But this is not how God sees us. As believers, we know there is "no condemnation for those who are in Christ Jesus" (Rom. 8:1). Are you on someone's bad side? No matter how hard you try, it's impossible to get on their good side. It might be because of your color, your gender, a mistake you made somewhere in the past, your personality, or a relationship you have with someone they consider an enemy. For one reason or another, you have already been judged, and there is no mercy.

These false views of God must be replaced with the truth. First, God is not uninterested in us. The belief that our performance is not good enough to evoke his attention is a lie. On the contrary, "God demonstrates his own love for us in this: While we were still sinners, Christ died for us" (Rom. 5:8). Long before we tried to perform for God, he became the performer, acting on our behalf, reaching out to get our attention.

God is not an unresponsive Father. He hears our prayers and protects us from evil. Listen to the words of Jesus:

> So I say to you: Ask and it will be given to you; seek and you will find; knock and the door will be opened to you. For everyone who asks receives; the one who seeks finds; and to the one who knocks, the door will be opened. Which of you fathers, if your son asks for a fish, will give him a snake instead? Or if he asks for an egg, will give him a scorpion? If you then, though you are evil, know how to give good gifts to your children, how much more will your Father in heaven give the Holy Spirit to those who ask him! (Luke 11:9–13)

We cannot control how and when God will respond, but we can trust that his response will be aligned with his will and in accordance with his timing.

Finally, God has been more than merciful to us, and we must be careful not to see God as an unrighteous judge. Jesus told the parable of such a judge to remind us that justice and mercy are at the forefront of his plan for earth.

> Then Jesus told his disciples a parable to show them that they should always pray and not give up. He said: "In a certain town there was a judge who neither feared God nor cared what people

thought. And there was a widow in that town who kept coming to him with the plea, 'Grant me justice against my adversary.' For some time he refused. But finally he said to himself, 'Even though I don't fear God or care what people think, yet because this widow keeps bothering me, I will see that she gets justice, so that she won't eventually come and attack me!'" And the Lord said, "Listen to what the unjust judge says. And will not God bring about justice for his chosen ones, who cry out to him day and night? Will he keep putting them off? I tell you, he will see that they get justice, and quickly. However, when the Son of Man comes, will he find faith on the earth?" (Luke 18:1–8)

In shared community, we have the responsibility to correct false views of God that inhibit our relationship with him. That is why earlier I discussed being a mirror of truth to one another. Suppose a friend makes a flippant comment, saying, "I wonder if God hears me at all!" As we approach this follower of Jesus, we must be tender and loving—and truthful. Let's affirm that God does hear her prayers and that we are a big part of the answer. He placed her in a loving community to walk with her through the pain and frustration, to lift her up when she gets down, and to serve her in her time of need.

A False View of Self

We also must let the truth get in the way of our false narratives about ourselves. The following examples detail several common misconceptions.

I am the center of the universe. If we are honest, we really do want the world to work according to our schedule, agenda, and expectations for success. It takes some hard-hitting redemptive truth to break that self-centered point of view and remind us of what we really are. In a world filled with rock stars, sports giants, business tycoons, personal achievement gurus, technology titans, and entertainment moguls, it is easy to get caught up in the it's-all-about-me syndrome.

Jesus told a story about a rich, self-absorbed farmer who had such abundance that he needed more room for his crops.

"This is what *I'll* do. *I* will tear down *my* barns and build bigger ones, and there *I* will store *my* surplus grain. And *I'll* say to *myself*, 'You have plenty of grain laid up for many years. Take life easy; eat, drink and be merry.'" But God said to him, "You fool! This very night your life will be demanded from you. Then who will get what you have prepared for yourself? This is how it will be with whoever stores up things for themselves but is not rich toward God." (Luke 12:18–21, italics mine)

I highlighted the personal pronouns to illustrate how self-centered the rich farmer was and to remind us how self-indulgent we also can be. Christ must move into our center and replace our self-adulation with heartfelt devotion to him. As he moves into that center position, we become interested in the needs of our community, not just our own.

I am unworthy of love, affection, and friendship. This shame-filled view of self produces depression, fear, withdrawal, and mistrust of others. In love, we must confront this view and allow the sword of truth to penetrate deeply, revealing the false narratives of shame and unworthiness. In the story of the Samaritan woman at the well (John 4), we find a beautiful picture of how the love of Jesus can break through shame and offer living water to a parched, battered soul. In love, Jesus revealed her checkered past and exposed her damaged heart. But then he offered healing grace, tender truth, and real hope. Above all, he offered himself.

In community, we remind one another that "Christ in us" pushes away our shame and guilt so that we can declare, "I am loved, I matter, and I am a friend of God."

A False View of Others

In our relationships around the table, we can embrace the truth so that we can replace our false view of others with a biblical view. It hurts to see our destructive patterns revealed, making us aware of how we treat others around us, even our closest friends and spouses. We must shine the light of truth on these false views so that ultimately we can be healed.

Others will hurt me if they have the chance. People with this view may have thoughts like the following:

> *The boss will give his best clients to other managers, not me.*
>
> *Dad will come home drunk again and hurt me, but I deserve it.*
>
> *My teacher is looking for ways to fail me in school.*
>
> *The cool kids will bully me, keeping me from their circle of friends.*
>
> *My spouse will always laugh at my dreams.*

When you hear these comments in community, it is important to probe more deeply and ask questions. This is why we must tell our stories and listen with empathy and real interest. What is it that is making this person fearful, skeptical, and cynical? Obviously, they have experienced deep hurts and wounds in the past, but they can be redeemed by the love of Christ and the support of our community.

Others will use me for their own purposes. Some years ago, I was asked to speak at a local business gathering about the role of faith in the context of work. The message was well received, and I enjoyed my time with the group. As I headed toward my car, a man followed me and said, "Excuse me. Do you have a minute?" I was glad to stop and listen to him. "A few years ago, I was involved in a business deal with a 'Christian' who was very public about his faith. As a result, I never questioned his motives or integrity when we were structuring the contracts. I had no reason to think anything might go wrong." I could see where this story was headed, and it wasn't going to end well. "Sadly, he had adjusted the numbers to give him a greater percentage of the earnings. I did not discover this until much later. It was awful." With obvious disappointment, he said very firmly and sadly, "I will never trust another 'Christian' businessman again."

We talked a few more moments, and I expressed my apologies and my grief about the situation. Inside, I hoped that someday a few people who love Christ would enter his life and reveal what real integrity looks like. He had been used and was wary of others using him again. From then on, he kept his cards close to his vest, took fewer risks, and avoided people he thought might hurt him—including God.

Others will reject me if I reach out to them. People with this view believe, "I don't deserve to be with those people, so I won't try." We fear reaching out to people we perceive are better or more successful than we are. At a company meeting, we don't shake hands with the new regional manager. We think a church leader is more spiritual than we are, so we don't even talk with her. As a result, we miss opportunities to serve, to grow, to build new relationships, to become more successful in our work, and to make spiritual progress.

Others do not understand me and do not want to help me. We believe, "My situation is so unique and my pain so severe that no one has ever experienced it." This is a common feeling in recovery groups when people attend their first meeting. It is easy to feel that our problems are unique and that no one has experienced the level of pain or betrayal or anxiety that we have. But as stories are shared at the table, we realize how much in common we have with one another. Others actually do understand our pain, our weaknesses, our frustrations, and our fears. They understand because they are human, and they too are broken.

People want to help us; they want a relationship with us. But we see ourselves as a failure and view others as flourishing, so we feel a sense of loss, grief, sadness, and isolation. But each of us is loved, and each of us has a contribution to make to the community. Others want to use their gifts to encourage us even as we use ours to serve them. That is how we share the grace of God with one another. "Each of you should use whatever gift you have received to serve others, as faithful stewards of God's grace in its various forms" (1 Pet. 4:10).

Amazingly, God's grace flows through us and into the lives of others when we claim the truth about our identity in Christ and serve one another. The Spirit of truth will help us to understand our value and remind us that we are loved. We are an object of God's love and a channel of his grace.

It may be painful to confront these false views—of God, self, and others—with truth from Scripture and feedback from our relationships. But God is in the business of transforming false narratives with his truth. He wants us to see him as a loving God, fully engaged in our lives. He wants us to see ourselves as chosen and beloved servants. He wants us to see others as people to be known and trusted. He wants to shape us into the image of Jesus.

Flawed Is the New Perfect

In November 2013, Carolyn Gregoire wrote an article in the *Huffington Post* titled "14 Signs Your Perfectionism Has Gotten out of Control," which includes the following:

You are highly critical of others—you tend to reject in others what you cannot accept in yourself.

You have a hard time opening up to people—you have to be strong and in control of yourself and your emotions.

You take everything personally—you do not bounce back from mistakes, you are beaten down by them.

You're never quite "there yet"—you are an overachiever and evaluate your worth by what you haven't done yet.

You get really defensive when criticized—you take control by defending yourself against any perceived threat.

You get secretly nostalgic for your school days—you found comfort in the structure and reward system of school.[2]

Gregoire then quotes author and researcher Brené Brown: "Perfectionism is not about striving for excellence or healthy striving. . . . It's . . . a way of thinking and feeling that says this: 'If I look perfect, do it perfect, work perfect and live perfect, I can avoid or minimize shame, blame and judgment.'"[3]

The Christian faith is designed for the perpetually flawed, not for passionate perfectionists. If we have no flaws, we don't need forgiveness, grace, or mercy. But many of us are perfectionists at heart, striving to please God in our own strength, trying to "be all that we can be," and feeling awful whenever we act like humans.

We read, "Be perfect . . . as your heavenly Father is perfect" (Matt. 5:48) and get right to work, only to fail within the first five minutes. But the verse does not say, "Do everything perfectly as your heavenly Father does everything perfectly." It is about *being*, not doing. We can *be* perfect, righteous, holy, and good because God has made us so by virtue of the shed blood of Christ. Our actions this side of heaven will never be perfect, but we are made perfect in Christ. What a relief!

Your imperfections are part of your story. Right now you might have a propensity to be judgmental or hypocritical or defensive or easily angered. If you are willing to let the truth do its work, to share and live in a circle of truth, those imperfections can be healed. Permanently? No. We will stumble and fall more times than we can count. But there is grace and mercy every step of the way. Affirming that both Jew and Gentile have sinned but also have been recipients of God's grace, Paul says, "For God has bound everyone over to disobedience so that he may have mercy on them all" (Rom. 11:32). Mercy on them all! That includes you and me. And that's good news.

But you do not have to do this courageous work. You can give in to fear and doubt, turn the other way, and simply avoid the entire process. Here are common tactics for avoiding our flaws:

Deny them: "I know how to keep a job; I just haven't found the job that fits me. The last five just were not designed for me."

Minimize them: "Really, I'm not angry! I just get a little frustrated at times. It's not that bad. You simply caught me on a rough day."

Medicate them: "I don't *need* this double Scotch. I just *enjoy* one sometimes after a stressful day at work. You would too if you had my boss."

Spiritualize them: "I'm just a sinner like everyone else. No one's perfect. All have sinned and fallen short. The Bible says we are jars of clay. I guess mine just has a few more cracks in it. God loves me just the way I am."

Don't portray a false self to the world. Face your flaws in the power of the Spirit. Show up as you really are and offer yourself to God's redeeming work through the Spirit of truth.

When we come together in the circle of truth and speak reality to one another, pain is inevitable. Truth can hurt, especially when it reveals our flaws and exposes our motives. A loving community, one in which we welcome one another to the table despite our flaws (indeed, because of our flaws) and pick up a towel with humility, need not fear the truth. The pain is real as the great Physician cuts away the damaged tissue and deadly tumors that ravage our souls. But then comes the healing, the result of grace dispensed by a tender Father and shared in a transformational community.

That is the truth we want, that is the truth we need. But not everyone agrees. For some, the truth is dangerous.

Truth Is Dangerous

Politics is my life, but not your run-of-the-mill political squabbling. Mine is far more radical. I use words like *overthrow*, *insurgency*, and *takeover*. Some people have social power while others have financial influence and strength or wield military might. But political power trumps them all. It's time for a shift in power, time to move Rome out and restore the kingdom of Israel.

At first I thought that was Jesus's intention. When he said, "The kingdom of heaven is at hand," I got excited, until I realized he was talking about a different kind of kingdom, one characterized by spiritual power. I wonder if we can use his spiritual supremacy to our advantage. With him on our side, we could conquer the world. He has no chance of doing that on his own.

Spiritual authority is exciting. When Jesus sent us out two by two—my partner was Judas Iscariot—the demons treated us like royalty. Nothing could stop us. There's got to be a way to harness that kind of energy for political purposes. But Jesus does not see it, and Judas, who I thought was going to join us, now has some kind of agenda of his own.

I know Jesus wants to change my ambitions. At times I believe he can. But we are making no progress. The authorities are threatening to shut us down, and we're not ready to confront them. If only we could gain control, then Jesus could move freely about and continue preaching, healing, and teaching. He chose me for his mission, but now I need him for mine. It is dangerous around here, but I am not afraid. I am willing to die for the cause. Jesus must know I would do the same for him. I have more energy than the other eleven put together. But his cause and my ambitions are butting heads.

For now, I will sit tight and see what unfolds. I must admit I enjoy being in this room. There's a sense of peace here. If only it would stay this way, I think I could be persuaded. Even tonight, despite all the uncertainty, I hang on his every word, and my passions are stirred again for his kingdom, for his mission. Things have to break one way or the other, and I want to be on the winning side.

One thing is certain: he won't find anyone with passion like mine. I am Simon the Zealot.

Danger: Truth at Work

I arrived at one of my favorite coffee shops to do some emailing and writing and noticed a small group of college students reading and discussing the Bible. I couldn't resist the opportunity. "You're not reading the Bible, are you? You have a lot of nerve reading that here in public. Are you with some kind of church or something? Do you really believe that stuff?" For a moment, the six of them sat stunned, caught off guard by my confrontational tone and demeanor.

"Um," stumbled one of them, "we are part of a youth and college ministry at our church, and we come here, um . . ."

I interrupted him mid-sentence. "You know that what you are reading is a very dangerous book, right? It has sure wrecked a lot of lives." I waited for a few moments as they looked at one another, still confused but not ashamed, still wondering what to say to this jerk who was interrupting them. "I know," I said, "because it sure has wrecked mine." Finally, I smiled the smile I'd been holding back. After a good laugh (and relief on the faces of a few!), we talked briefly, and I encouraged them in their ministry.

Truth can be a dangerous thing, especially in the wrong hands. It was true in Jesus's day, and two thousand years later things are not much different. The Bible is a dangerous book. That's because our God is a dangerous God. Annie Dillard captures the idea:

> It is madness to wear ladies' straw hats and velvet hats to church; we should all be wearing crash helmets. Ushers should issue life preservers and signal flares; they should lash us to our pews. For the sleeping god may wake someday and take offense, or the waking god may draw us out to where we can never return.[1]

Are we willing to encounter the dangerous God of truth? Are we willing to face burning bushes and pillars of fire? Or do we prefer a kindly heavenly Father, a domesticated Jesus, and a cuddly Holy Spirit?

Reality Check

Here's the truth about the truth: it was never meant to be barricaded in a stained-glass church or kept under wraps between the pages of a leather-bound, gold-embossed book where it's predictable and manageable. It was meant to run free and wild, to shake the heavens and rock the earth. We should never be bored with God's truth. Brennan Manning warns us concerning our propensity to package God and reduce his fiery truth to mere theological propositions: "Instead of expanding our capacity for life, joy, and mystery, religion often contradicts it. As systematic theology advances, the sense of wonder declines."[2] That last phrase terrifies me. I teach at a Christian college and seminary. Do I enjoy talking about God more than I enjoy God himself? Has my passion for truth degenerated into a passion for theology?

An email from a friend makes this distinction even more profoundly. He compares "knowing about God" and "knowing God," and I have summarized the outcomes of the two in a chart that I use in my teaching. It serves as a reminder for me more than for my students.

Knowledge about God	Knowing God
Leads to pride	Leads to humility
Leads to indifference	Leads to passion
Leads to arrogance	Leads to sincerity
Leads to respect	Leads to love
Leads to control of others	Leads to abandonment
Defines God	Reveals God
Provides correction	Produces surrender
Judges others	Convicts us

Our impulse to confine God and control his teachings flows from our deepest fear—the fear we might have to change. And we hate change, unless it is on our terms.

In our men's group, I once asked, "Is it possible to experience real transformation after fifty years of age, or are we stuck with our undesirable habits and patterns forever?" It was an uncomfortable question, to say the least. The responses indicated I had touched a nerve, and they kicked off a stimulating discussion, prompting me to wonder whether I really *want* to change. I had to ask myself, "Am I more enamored with the idea of change than I am with change itself? Is the prospect of change an exciting topic for group conversation, or is it something to which I am willing to commit my life no matter how demanding?"

This I know: there is no real transformation without truth, and without truth there is no real possibility of forging a vibrant community. We must surrender to truth, yet when we do so we place our fragile selves in the hands of the author of truth. That is good news. But here's the bad news: his mission is *not* to protect us from harm and shield us from danger. If we believe otherwise, we are resting in the wrong hands.

This is why truth is dangerous. We must set aside all presumptions of personal security and safety when we place our lives in truthful hands. Speaking to our need for transformation and the reality of God's call for our unconditional surrender to his life-changing mission, Manning reveals the challenge to comply:

> There is a power available to transcend our automatic emotional responses and robot-like behavior. Endowed with the courage

to risk everything on the truth of the gospel, we surrender our gnawing need to be okay and cease applying spiritual cosmetics to make ourselves presentable.

And yet . . . the prospect frightens us. We'd like to stay close enough to the fire to keep warm but are reluctant to dive in. We know we will come out burnt, incandescently transformed. Life never will be the same again. Nonetheless, we are dissatisfied with the narrow dimensions of our partial commitment.[3]

This struggle is all too familiar to many of us. So what do we do?

Highway to the Danger Zone

When Ernest Shackleton recruited explorers for his trans-Antarctic expedition in the early 1900s, he placed this ad in the paper:

> Men wanted for hazardous journey . . . small wages, bitter cold, long months of complete darkness, constant danger. Safe return doubtful. Honor and recognition in case of success.[4]

I'm sure you wanted to sign on as quickly as I. But let's think for a moment. Is it much different from the call to follow Christ wherever he may lead? Let's rewrite the ad:

> Wanted: men and women for hazardous spiritual (and perhaps physical) adventure. Requires total surrender to expedition leader, daily cross bearing, likely ridicule, and possible betrayal. Self-sacrifice and humility essential. Potential loss of friends, loss of job, and loss of income. May require dramatic changes in career path, housing, transportation, and financial

232

status. Pays no wages but will cost you 10 percent or more of your current annual income. Success is certain, recognition is assured, and rewards are guaranteed (but distributed only after death).

Shackleton had no intention of misleading potential followers. He presented a daunting snapshot of this high-risk journey before asking men to sign on. Jesus communicated similar sentiments when he sent his disciples on their first ministry expedition to preach and heal (in Matt. 10 and Luke 10). We hardly speak with that kind of conviction today. Our call to salvation is rarely accompanied by a call to surrender anything of substance. That sounds too dangerous and too intimidating, and we have seats to fill and goals to reach. So we describe the benefits of saying yes to Jesus—forgiveness of sin, freedom from guilt and shame, eternal life, membership in the body of Christ, joy everlasting—and ignore the sacrifices and commitments that accompany joining the Master on his mission. Imagine Shackleton promising nothing but rewards and the joys of adventurous exploration without communicating the harsh realities that accompanied Arctic travel in the early 1900s. It would have sounded like an Alaskan cruise rather than a rigorous foray into the unknown tundra.

We must come to grips with the danger of truth for ourselves before calling others to the mission. Are we willing to embrace the truth, practice it, teach it, and live with the results? Or will we go along only if we can choose the truths we enjoy, like children at a hotel brunch grabbing goodies from the dessert bar? Are the members of our community willing to help one another make real commitments to the gospel—to the poor, the orphan, the widow, and the stranger? Are we willing to live the good news even when those around us find our way of life offensive or foolish? (I do not mean the foolish and offensive things Christians do that are unrelated to the truth.) Truth cuts deeply into culture, encouraging some hearers and enraging others. This brings us to a final aspect of truth we must acknowledge.

Not everyone likes the truth.

Enemies of Truth

Our community has adversaries. We don't need to make enemies—they already exist. I want to highlight three specific enemies that will attack our community as we seek to become a circle of truth. Let's confront them as a community. Let's lock arms and guard one another from these enemies.

Enemy #1: The Evil One

From the very beginning, the perpetrator of evil determined to destroy any semblance of loving, redemptive community in the world. His primary strategy—to divide and conquer—was first deployed in the garden against the first family. He remains active today, setting brother against brother, family against family, and nation against nation. He leaves mangled marriages, fractured families, broken businesses, and conflict-ridden countries in his destructive wake. And he takes great pleasure in doing so. He was defeated at the cross but remains influential in the world. His ultimate destruction will come at the end of the age, but until then we would be fools to ignore the spiritual battle that rages, sometimes hidden from our eyes. Jesus understood the seriousness of this conflict when he prayed on the eve of his arrest:

> I have given them your word and the world has hated them, for they are not of the world any more than I am of the world. My prayer is not that you take them out of the world but that you protect them from the evil one. (John 17:14–15)

Notice the focus of Jesus's prayer. He does not say, "Protect them from illness; keep them from disease; guard them against injuries." Instead, he prays for protection from the divisive power of evil because the evil one hates community. In community, we are powerful, faithful, and truthful. Destroy that community and you remove a great force for justice and mercy in our world.

Perhaps to our disappointment, Jesus does not pray that we be removed from the evil in the world. We remain in the world as salt and light, as champions of God's love, grace, and forgiveness. Removing us from the world would mean removing us as Spirit-empowered agents for healing, goodness, kindness, and hope. So God leaves us here to do his will on earth, as it is in heaven. But while we're in the world, we are combatants in the spiritual conflict that rages here.

That is why the Bible urges, "Make every effort to keep the unity of the Spirit through the bond of peace" (Eph. 4:3). It takes effort to stand against evil, and part of that effort is praying together as a community. Listen to what Paul says two chapters later in Ephesians to a church that was in danger of division and of losing her first love, Jesus (see Rev. 2:4, where John confronts the church at Ephesus):

> Finally, be strong in the Lord and in his mighty power. Put on the full armor of God, so that you can take your stand against the devil's schemes. For our struggle is not against flesh and blood, but against the rulers, against the authorities, against the powers of this dark world and against the spiritual forces of evil in the heavenly realms. . . . Stand firm then, with the belt of truth buckled around your waist, with the breastplate of righteousness in place, and with your feet fitted with the readiness that comes from the gospel of peace. In addition to all this, take up the shield of faith, with which you can extinguish all the flaming arrows of the evil one. Take the helmet of salvation and the sword of the Spirit, which is the word of God. And pray in the Spirit on all occasions with all kinds of prayers and requests. With this in mind, be alert and always keep on praying for all the Lord's people. (Eph. 6:10–12, 14–18)

Note that last exhortation: "Always keep on praying for all the Lord's people." Pray for unity and protection from the evil one. Our flock of followers has more power and impact on this world than we can imagine. We cannot underestimate our power. The evil one certainly does not.

Enemy #2: Legalism

Legalism and grace have been battling it out ever since the fall of humankind. And we will see vestiges of that battle in our community. Henry Cloud has been helpful in assisting us to understand grace versus legalism. The chart below summarizes his teaching.[5]

	Legalism-Based Theology	Grace-Based Theology
Promoted by	Control-oriented groups and churches	Recovery groups and grace-oriented churches
Membership requirement	You must appear "good" to get in	You must admit you are "bad" (sinful) to get in
Terms used for failure	Backslider, not enough faith, not enough effort	Denial of truth, unwilling to face reality
What happens as a result	Outwardly alive, dead inside—Pharisees	Outwardly dead, filled with life, humility, and growth—New Testament Christians

Legalists use compliance with manmade rules and measurements as an indicator of spiritual growth and maturity. Conversely, Jesus focuses on the condition of the heart and the actions (not simply words) that demonstrate fruitfulness and faithfulness.

A tree is recognized by its fruit. (Matt. 12:33)

Woe to you, teachers of the law and Pharisees, you hypocrites! You are like whitewashed tombs, which look beautiful on the outside but on the inside are full of the bones of the dead and everything unclean. (Matt. 23:27)

Recently on YouTube I watched a popular theologian commend the church where he was speaking because they had a large, permanent pulpit built into the platform rather than a portable, removable one. He concluded that this church must surely value the preaching of the Word of God, while other churches must have a weak view of preaching, as evidenced by their Plexiglas pulpits, which are easily removed from the platform.

What an absolutely silly assumption. I wondered about the apostle Paul's "portable pulpit," about the churches I visited in destitute villages in South Africa and in the slums of Guatemala, about churches that gather in homes in China (like the first churches), about churches that meet in theaters or storefronts in inner cities. Few churches in the world could ever afford a permanent pulpit, let alone the one he was pointing to, regardless of how much they value preaching.

Legalism thrives when people pass judgment about the character and attitude of others based on outward appearances or the performance of approved rituals. Imagine another guest preacher the following week saying, "Look at this gaudy pulpit! Any church that spends so much money to build a pulpit like this must not care about the poor. I am so grateful for churches with portable pulpits because they obviously spend more money helping people than building pulpits!"

When members of a community judge one another solely on a few facts, outward appearances, or brief remarks, legalism raises its ugly head. Snap judgments and snide remarks—and the body language that goes with them—start to multiply, and someone (hopefully you) needs to call legalism out. If you are in a small group, consider spending a few sessions on the Sermon on the Mount in Matthew 5–7, allowing the truth to inform your attitudes and comments.

Where legalism abounds, truthful speech and attitudes are considered subversive. When members of a community give the benefit of the doubt to one another, practice forgiveness, laugh at one another's quirks, and refrain from haughty judgments, legalists get irritated. You may hear them making statements such as "We need more tough love" or "There's a time for punishment, and this is the time"; you may even observe "sin lists" in their theology. No one uses the term, but everyone has a sin list.

The top four sins on the list—adultery, homosexuality, pornography, and abortion—are usually followed by drinking, drugs, smoking, stealing, lying, and foul language. A number of sins rarely or never make the list: pride, anger, gluttony, racism, ignorance of the poor, condescending language, gossip, slander, neglect of family, judging others, watching too much television, playing too much poker (a little poker is OK if you use Monopoly money and don't smoke cigars), spending too much time on the boat or on the golf course or shopping, leveraging questionable tax loopholes, and so on.

Everyone has a list. Once you have a list, you can prioritize sins (always place yours at the bottom) and assign a penalty for each. In this way, you can certify there is never "too much grace" or "too little law" going around.

A popular pastor was recently disciplined after many years of inappropriate behavior. Why did it take so long? Because his sins were not among the four or five "big ones." His included condescending comments about gays, inappropriate remarks about women, regular expressions of arrogance, power mongering, finger-pointing, plagiarism, and rudeness. I'm being sarcastic to make a point. For many years people dismissed his faults, doing a grave disservice to this pastor; he needed loving correction for his own growth and maturity.

Everyone in our community probably has a sin list. While we are not called to ignore wrongdoing, it is always easier to see the sins of others than our own. Self-examination within a community, rather than constant vigilance over the lives of others, makes for healthier relationships and, ironically, holier living by everyone. Conversely, pointing our fingers at others achieves exactly the opposite result—greater hypocrisy, self-righteousness, and illicit behavior.

Enemy #3: Unresolved Conflict

Facing conflict is productive; avoiding conflict is destructive.

A few years ago, a leader made some comments about me behind my back. He misrepresented statements I'd made about a ministry strategy and clearly wanted to paint me in a bad light to my supervisors. What's worse, this occurred twice in a short time frame. I discovered this kind of behavior was a pattern in his life, especially when he wanted to assert or preserve institutional power.

I overlooked the first offense, trying to give him the benefit of the doubt. (Perhaps he had misunderstood my statements, and there was no intent to cause harm.) After the second occurrence, I called and scheduled a meeting. I followed a biblical approach in confronting the problem, spoke the truth in love, and offered to move forward in our work environment with better understanding. He was defensive, deflected any truth about his wrongful behavior, made excuses, and sat there without expression. When I asked if he would please refrain from talking behind my back and come to me directly, he simply stared and sipped his coffee—no apologies, no responsibility for his actions.

The toughest time was the period between the offenses. The unresolved situation ate away at me. When I scheduled the meeting, I knew it was affecting him, even though he could not put words to it. Unresolved conflict is worse than a poorly navigated conflict resolution. Though the attempt may be imperfect, at least you gave it a try and probably made some progress. Poorly resolved conflict may dent the ego, but unresolved conflict damages the heart.

Let's highlight a few principles and tactics to guide you in conflict resolution. First of all, the Bible places a high value on speaking the truth in love (Eph. 4) and on dealing with relational breakdown as soon as possible (Matt. 5:23–26; 18:15–18). Jesus places a high premium on conflict resolution because he places a high value on community. His church—the ultimate community—cannot afford to have destructive people with unresolved conflicts running amok. If not confronted with integrity, conflict can split a church and shred even the most durable of friendships. But what does it look like to confront conflict in a community?

Before we talk details, here is a general principle to follow: if the conflict happens in the community, deal with it as a community. For example, at a small group, Allison shares her frustration with two managers she supervises. She wants to deal with the situation with integrity, but she gets easily frustrated and angry. As she describes the situation to the group, Mike blurts out, "Maybe you just can't strong-arm the guys at work like you do the gals." Obviously, this is a glaring, inappropriate remark that reeks of sexism and sarcasm. The group cannot ignore the comment or remove the damage done, but they can act as a mirror. A member might say, "I think we all felt the edge of that remark, Mike. Did you really mean what you said? It sounded like you were talking down to her, and I know that made me feel uncomfortable." Next, the group needs to talk through the conflict together. While the situation may not be resolved at this point—Mike and Allison will likely need to sit down and do some repair work on their relationship—the group has played a role. A few more tips for conflict resolution follow.

First, act but don't *react*. Reacting means acting immediately instead of waiting a short time to gather thoughts, pray, and allow emotions to run their course. When emotions run high, words tend to fly, so wait twenty-four to forty-eight hours before responding. In the case above, a brief interaction by the group was appropriate, but then there needs to be time before the real work of engaging in a difficult conversation begins.

Second, meet face-to-face. Never use email, texting, or letters to resolve conflict. Most of our emotions and feelings cannot be conveyed in writing. You need to look into the other person's eyes to see what the person is feeling and how they are responding to your comments.

Third, affirm the relationship. Make genuine comments about your desire to maintain and build this relationship. Describe examples from the past that indicate how important the relationship is and why it matters. For example, someone might say, "Mike, we often appreciate how you speak boldly to defend the weak in our community and how you pray earnestly for God to work in your life. That means a lot to us." These kinds of genuine comments remind Mike he is cared about and loved, even though you must confront his behavior. The adage "Be hard on the issue but soft on the person" expresses the attitude you should strive for.

Fourth, make observations, not accusations. For Allison to say "Mike, you're just jealous because I am a woman with a position of authority" is unproductive and puts Mike on the defensive. It only adds fuel to the fire. Instead, she could say, "Mike, I am saddened and hurt by what you said. The remark had sexist implications and a very sarcastic tone. It sounded like you were making judgments about how I relate to my employees. Is that what I heard?" Speak truth without throwing another grenade into the fray.

Fifth, listen and learn. After you speak your version of the truth, listen, get some facts, and clarify what each party understands. In this step, you are basically communicating, "I have made my comments; now I want to hear from you. Did you hear and understand what I was saying? Now help me to hear and understand your response." Get it all on the table. In the bestselling work *Crucial Conversations*, the authors explain:

> When it comes to risky, controversial, and emotional conversations, skilled people find a way to get all relevant information (from themselves and others) out into the open.
>
> That's it. At the core of every successful conversation lies the free flow of relevant information. People openly and honestly express their opinions, share their feelings, and articulate their theories. They willingly and capably share their views, even when their ideas are controversial or unpopular.[6]

Finally, after all the facts and feelings are on the table, work toward a resolution (solving the problem) and reconciliation (restoring the relationship). The former is easier than the latter. But be sure to explain what you each want. In other words, what does reconciliation look like to everyone involved? Make no assumptions. Be clear.

Do others believe I care about their goals in this conversation?

Do they trust my motives?

What do I want for me?

What do I want for others?

What do I want for the relationship?[7]

Depending on the extent of the damage and the nature of the relationship, it may take time for the people involved to return to normal and rebuild a level of trust. While there may be forgiveness and understanding, the friendship may need to be reformulated or repurposed. Time may heal the fracture, but the relationship may be different.

Truth is dangerous because it comes with great power. When used wisely and with courage, truth can be a tool for transformation. But when used maliciously, it can become a spiritual weapon of mass destruction.

Coming Full Circle

Our hunger for truth is satisfied only when we live in a circle of truth. There we find satisfaction and nourishment for our souls and mutual encouragement to face the hard realities of life. Truth cuts to our core and does its transforming, healing work so that we can share it and practice it with others in our community. But living in the truth is not easy and is sometimes quite dangerous. So we walk by faith, trusting God and living in the power of the Spirit to make our way and fulfill God's will.

This transforming circle is a powerful entity, and many people long to become a part of such a community if we will simply invite them.

Conclusion

Becoming an Answer to Prayer

We come to the table with hope and a longing to connect. There we discover we belong and begin doing life together in community. We grab a towel because the Master did the same, and we serve others and give ourselves fully to the ministry for which he has commissioned us. We give ourselves to the world in joy and love while remembering that our health as a community is the strength from which we serve.

In the process, we strengthen our circle of community with truth—about God, about ourselves, and about others. We embrace reality with courage and hope, and we honestly face the truth and diligently practice a life of truth—individually and as a community.

As we do this, we discover we did not create our community. It is a gift given to us in which we participate and for which Christ prayed and died. On that Thursday evening, after sharing the

Passover meal with the Eleven, Jesus headed to Gethsemane and ultimately to Golgotha. The prospect of his certain arrest, beating, trial, and crucifixion drove him to his knees in prayer. Some call this the garden prayer, the one in which he asked the Father that, if possible, this cup of suffering might pass. But his desire to do the Father's will and accomplish our redemption outweighed his gut-wrenching longing to forego the entire ordeal. It was too much to bear, but he bore it nonetheless.

Yet, there was another prayer to be prayed, before Gethsemane. While the garden prayer was passionately personal, offered alone to the Father with the disciples listening at a distance (when they were not sleeping!), the prayer before it was a table prayer—a communal plea offered in their presence to encourage them, teach them, and reveal his heart for their community and for the world. What was the focus of this prayer? What did he pray for so intensely that even the impending cruelty of the whip and torture of the cross could not remove it from his heart? What was his concern in this impassioned plea to his Father?

Hear the cry of Jesus on the eve of his crucifixion:

I will remain in the world no longer, but they are still in the world, and I am coming to you. *Holy Father, protect them by the power of your name, the name you gave me, so that they may be one as we are one.* While I was with them, I protected them and kept them safe by that name you gave me. None has been lost except the one doomed to destruction so that Scripture would be fulfilled.

I am coming to you now, but I say these things while I am still in the world, so that they may have the full measure of my joy within them. I have given them your word and the world has hated them, for they are not of the world any more than I am of the world. My prayer is not that you take them out of the world but that you protect them from the evil one. They are not of the world, even as I am not of it. Sanctify them by the truth; your word is truth. As you sent me into the world, I have sent them into the world. For them I sanctify myself, that they too may be truly sanctified.

My prayer is not for them alone. I pray also for those who will believe in me through their message, that all of them may be one, Father, just as you are in me and I am in you. May they also be in us so that the world may believe that you have sent me. I have given them the glory that you gave me, that they may be one as we are one—I in them and you in me—so that they may be brought to complete unity. Then the world will know that you sent me and have loved them even as you have loved me. (John 17:11–23, italics mine)

At the beginning of the prayer, verses 1–5, the primary focus is on Jesus's work as he completes his mission and glorifies the Father. But by verse 6, the prayer concerns his disciples and then, by verse 20, all who will eventually believe in his name. What is the focus? People. And what does Jesus passionately desire above all else for these people over whom he prays?

That they would be one.

Oneness.

Jesus brought his followers to the table, he picked up a towel, and then he spoke the truth, inviting them to do the same. With the ordeal of the cross just hours away, he prays that they will live this table-towel-truth life in oneness as a committed community of Christ followers.

247

Why? Here's the payoff. Look at verse 23 again: "that they may be brought to complete unity. Then the world will know that you sent me and have loved them even as you have loved me." He prays for unity so that the world will know. Our community is the greatest tool at our disposal for sharing the good news of Jesus with the world. Certainly, believers must thoughtfully and skillfully articulate the facts of the faith, answering the questions of critics and strengthening the beliefs of the faithful. We must "always be prepared to give an answer to everyone who asks [us] to give the reason for the hope that [we] have. But [we should] do this with gentleness and respect" (1 Pet. 3:15). And we must preach and teach the Word, serve the poor, and stand strong in the face of persecution or ridicule. But we were never supposed to do all this alone. Before we give an answer, we can be the answer. As we speak the Word, we can practice the Word—together.

In the community of Jesus, no one stands alone. This is the cry of his heart and the passion of his prayer. Gilbert Bilezikian is a mentor and friend, the primary vision caster and cofounding elder of Willow Creek Community Church, where I served for eighteen years. Dr. B. (as we affectionately call him) wrote the following in his landmark book *Community 101* concerning Jesus's prayer in John 17:

> The oneness that Jesus was praying for was not mere unity. It was the oneness that reaches deep into the being of God and finds its source in the relation between Father and Son. Jesus was asking for the restoration among humans of the oneness that had originally been entrusted to them in creation, a oneness made in the image of the oneness within the Trinity. . . .

Christ's concern for oneness in his last prayer was not limited to his immediate disciples. It extended to all believers of all times throughout the future of the church. . . .

This concern for the survival of the church down through the ages provides the explanation for the anguished tones of Jesus' prayer. He knew that if the church should fail to demonstrate community to the world, it would fail to accomplish its mission because the world would have reason to disbelieve the gospel (vv. 21, 23). According to that prayer, the most convincing proof of the truth of the gospel is the perceptible oneness of his followers.

Dr. B. now drives the point all the way home:

In our day, whenever the church is ineffective and its witness remains unproductive, the first questions that must be raised are whether the church functions as authentic community and whether it lives out the reality of its oneness. In a community-starved world, the most potent means of witness to the truth of the gospel is the magnetic power of the oneness that was committed by Christ to his new community at the center of history.[1]

We need to return to our communal roots. We need to recapture the community-driven spirit of the early church and practice being the church for the world. It is clear we have lost our focus and stand the risk of losing our impact. One person said it quite profoundly: "In Jerusalem, Christianity was a lifestyle. In Rome it became an institution, in Europe it became a culture, and it America it has become an enterprise."[2]

A popular saying referring to Jesus's death and our salvation states, "When he was on the cross, you were on his mind."

249

While it's memorable and there's truth in it, this catchy phrase serves primarily to remind us of our personal redemption and our individual relationship with Christ. Hours before the cross, however, you and I and the whole world were definitely on his mind, in his heart, and on his lips. The people of God—his emerging church, the community of the table-towel-truth—were the focus of his prayer. And it should be the focus of ours. It is time to rediscover the lifestyle of community. It is time again to become people of the Way.

Pray to that end, as Jesus prayed. Pray that we would all be one as he and the Father and the Spirit are one. Pray that our oneness will serve as a bold declaration of love, reconciliation, salvation, peace, and hope to a fractured, broken, disconnected world that desperately needs to be restored to its creation-designed oneness. Pray as Jesus prayed.

Pray for oneness.

Notes

Introduction: A Personal Invitation

1. Dietrich Bonhoeffer, *Life Together* (San Francisco: Harper & Row, 1954), 30.

Part 1: Join the Fellowship of the Table

1. Jean Vanier, *Community and Growth* (Mahwah, NJ: Paulist Press, 1979), 3.

Chapter 1: Finding Your Place at the Table

1. Neal Krause and M. Wulff Keith, "Church-Based Social Ties, a Sense of Belonging in a Congregation, and Physical Health Status," *International Journal for the Psychology of Religion* 15, no. 1 (2005): 73–93.

2. Mark Thomsen, "Reflections on the Priority of Belonging," *Currents in Theology and Mission* 31, no. 4 (August 2004): 318.

3. Brennan Manning, *A Glimpse of Jesus: A Stranger to Self-Hatred* (San Francisco: HarperCollins, 2003), 55, 57.

4. Richard Flory and Donald E. Miller, *Finding Faith: The Spiritual Quest of the Post-Boomer Generation* (New Brunswick, NJ: Rutgers University Press, 2008), 145.

Chapter 2: Table Manners

1. David W. McMillan and David M. Chavis, "Sense of Community: A Definition and Theory," *Journal of Community Psychology* 14 (January 1986): 6–23.

2. Vanier, *Community and Growth*, 266.

3. Ibid. (italics in original).

4. Philip Yancey, "Lessons from Rock Bottom," *Christianity Today*, July 2000, 72 (italics in original).

5. M. Scott Peck, *The Road Less Travelled* (New York: Simon & Schuster, 1978), 44.

6. John 13:34; Galatians 5:13; 6:2; James 5:16.

7. Vanier, *Community and Growth*, 35–36.

8. Bethany Blankley, "Murder and Forgiveness: A Tale of Befriending a Brother's Killer," *Christian Post*, May 8, 2013, selected excerpts. For full story, see www.christianpost.com.

9. Vanier, *Community and Growth*, 37–38.

10. Adapted from Al-Anon. I have added the words "strive for" to the slogan.

11. See http://penguinproject.org for more information.

Chapter 3: Choose a Table, Any Table

1. For a few resources, see the "Conflict" chapters in the following: J. Dan Rothwell, *In Mixed Company: Communicating in Small Groups and Teams*, 5th ed. (Belmont, CA: Wadsworth, 2004); John F. Cragan, Chris R. Kasch, and David W. Wright, *Communication in Small Groups: Theory, Process, Skills*, 7th ed. (Boston: Wadsworth, 2009); and Lawrence R. Frey and J. Kevin Barge, eds., *Managing Group Life: Communicating in Decision-Making Groups* (Boston: Houghton Mifflin, 1997), 104–30.

2. Larry Crabb, *The Safest Place on Earth* (Nashville: Word, 1999), 40, 49.

3. Parker Palmer, *To Know as We Are Known: Education as a Spiritual Journey* (San Francisco: Harper, 1983), 69.

4. Parker Palmer, *To Know as We Are Known: Education as a Spiritual Journey* (San Francisco: HarperSanFrancisco, 1993), 8.

5. Heather Zempel, *Community Is Messy* (Downers Grove, IL: InterVarsity, 2012), 43–44.

Chapter 4: Table Tales

1. Dan Allender, *To Be Told* (Colorado Springs: WaterBrook, 2005), 39–40.

2. Ibid., 40.

3. See Luke 15, where heaven explodes with joy when just one sinner repents!

4. For a longer version, I recommend Scot McKnight, *The King Jesus Gospel* (Grand Rapids: Zondervan, 2011), a thorough, readable explanation of God's story.

5. Adapted from conference handout, Ralph Neighbour (Houston: Touch Outreach Ministries, 1992).

Part 2: Practice the Ministry of the Towel

1. Philippians 2:6–7 reads "although" in NASB and "though" in ESV and NLT.

2. Gerald F. Hawthorne and Ralph P. Martin, *Philippians*, rev. ed., Word Biblical Commentary 43 (Nashville: Thomas Nelson, 2004), comments on Phil. 2:5–11.

Chapter 5: Your Towel Has a Name on It

1. Rodney Stark, *The Rise of Christianity* (San Francisco: Harper, 1997), 83.

2. Rodney Clapp, *A Peculiar People* (Downers Grove, IL: InterVarsity, 1996).

3. Brennan Manning, *The Signature of Jesus* (Colorado Springs: Multnomah, 1996), 37, 55.

4. Isaiah 42–53 is often called the song of the Suffering Servant because it prophetically describes the coming of the Messiah and the death he would die for his people.

5. Brad Edwards, "Suburban Mom Dies Rescuing Child from Drowning," *CBS Chicago Online*, July 24, 2014, http://chicago.cbslocal.com/2014/07/24/suburban-mom-dies-rescuing-child-from-drowning/.

6. Vanier, *Community and Growth*, 89.

Chapter 6: A Dirty Towel Is a Happy Towel

1. Manning, *Glimpse of Jesus*, 125.

2. Ibid.

3. Ibid., 123.

Chapter 7: Arranging Our Towels in a Circle

1. Look at the counsel Jethro gives Moses in Exod. 18:17–23.

2. Vanier, *Community and Growth*, 212–13.

3. Ibid., 213.

4. John Stott, *The Cross of Christ* (Downers Grove, IL: InterVarsity, 1986), 271, 275, 277–78, 278.

5. Ibid., 285.

6. James Bryan Smith, *The Good and Beautiful Community* (Downers Grove, IL: InterVarsity, 2010), 129.

7. Ibid.

8. Ibid., 130–31.

Chapter 8: Don't Throw In the Towel

1. Henri Nouwen, *Life of the Beloved: Spiritual Living in a Secular World* (New York: Crossroad, 1995), 61.

2. Lance Witt, *Replenish: Leading from a Healthy Soul* (Grand Rapids: Baker, 2011), 23 (italics in original).

3. Nouwen, *Life of the Beloved*, 63.

4. John Ortberg, *The Me I Want to Be* (Grand Rapids: Zondervan, 2010), 190.

5. Brennan Manning, *Abba's Child* (Colorado Springs: NavPress, 2002), 46.

6. Todd Hunter, *Christianity beyond Belief: Following Jesus for the Sake of Others* (Downers Grove, IL: InterVarsity, 2009).

Chapter 9: A Hunger for Truth

1. Merrill Tenney, *Gospel of John*, Expositors Bible Commentary (Grand Rapids: Zondervan, 1991), 157–58.

2. Ibid., 158 (parenthetical addition is mine).

Chapter 10: Telling Ourselves the Truth

1. Richard Lamoreaux, "The Mirror Is a Liar," *PoetrySoup*, accessed January 14, 2015, http://www.poetrysoup.com/poem/the_mirror_is_a_liar_451788.

2. Quoted in Martin H. Manser, ed., *The Westminster Collection of Christian Quotations* (Louisville: Westminster John Knox, 2001), 20.

3. John 13:16, 20, 21, 38; 14:12; 16:7, 20, 23. Of all twenty-seven uses of the phrase in the New Testament, NIV translation, John uses it twenty-six times, including the eight referenced here.

4. Nouwen, *Life of the Beloved*, 62.

5. Henry Cloud and John Townsend, *Making Small Groups Work* (Grand Rapids: Zondervan, 2003), 206–7.

6. Manning, *Signature of Jesus*, 101–2.

Chapter 11: The Truth Hurts, the Truth Heals

1. Henry Cloud and I created this material together and delivered it in a variety of settings, individually and together, including at a church conference in Germany.

2. Carolyn Gregoire, "14 Signs Your Perfectionism Has Gotten out of Control," *Huffington Post*, November 6, 2013, http://www.huffingtonpost.com/2013/11/06/why-perfectionism-is-ruin_n_4212069.html.

3. Ibid.

Chapter 12: Truth Is Dangerous

1. Annie Dillard, *Teaching a Stone to Talk* (New York: Harper & Row, 1982), 52–53.

2. Manning, *Abba's Child*, 77.

3. Manning, *Signature of Jesus*, 186.

4. Martin Dugard, *The Explorers: A Study of Fearless Outcasts, Blundering Geniuses, and Impossible Success* (New York: Simon & Schuster, 2014), 96.

5. Teaching by Bill Donahue and Henry Cloud, Church Communications Network broadcast, 2006.

6. Kerry Patterson, Joseph Grenny, Ron McMillan, and Al Switzler, *Crucial Conversations: Tools for Talking When Stakes Are High*, 2nd ed. (New York: McGraw Hill, 2012), 23.

7. Ibid., 77–78.

Conclusion: Becoming an Answer to Prayer

1. Gilbert Bilezikian, *Community 101* (Grand Rapids: Zondervan, 1997), 36–37.

2. Conference handout, Ralph Neighbour (Houston: Touch Outreach Ministries, 1993).

Connect with

DR. BILL DONAHUE

o o o

Visit

drbilldonahue.com for:

- blog posts
- videos
- leadership-development resources
- and more!